Acknowledgements

With deep gratitude I offer this sincere thank-you to so many supportive folks in my life. To my husband, Rob Mahedy, for his unfaltering assistance and support to me during the writing of this book, and for riding every single trail in this book with me. To my folks, Roy and Loretta, for supporting me in living an outdoor lifestyle and teaching me the beauty of nature. To all my wonderful friends who have encouraged me through this process, and who I get to enjoy the great outdoors with! To Gene Bollig, for being so patient and helpful and doing such a fine job of designing this book. To Peter Vanags of Thin Air Software for being so careful and complete in mapping the region for this book. To all the organizations and individuals who work so hard to keep our trails open and in good shape, you are all doing a great job! Thanks to all the bike shops in Summit County and Vail for offering great information, support and service, to all mountain bikers. To Mike Zobbe and the Summit Fat Tire Society for information and help, and for keeping Summit County Trails open and in great shape. To the various individuals within the U.S. Forest Service for trails upkeep and for offering much information to me as well. To the Summit County and Breckenridge Open Space and Trails departments for all their work keeping trails and access open, and improving and signing trails. To the individual property owners who allow access to trails. To the individuals at Copper Mountain, Keystone, Vail, Beaver Creek and Breckenridge Ski Resorts for all their information on trails and for offering great photos for the book. To B & B Printers in Gunnison for doing a great job of putting this book together. And finally, to all those folks who purchase and use this book, I hope you have wonderful adventures using it!! You all have a part in this book.

Cover Photo by Jack Affleck, Vail Mountain
Inside Front Cover Photo by Jack Affleck, Commando Ridge
Inside Back Cover by Holly Annala, Buffeher Trail
Back Cover Photo by Leisa Gibson, The Ranch Trail

Graphic Design by Gene Bollig
Printing by B&B Printers, Gunnison, CO
Maps by Peter Vanags

©2005 • Holly Annala

AREA OVERVIEW

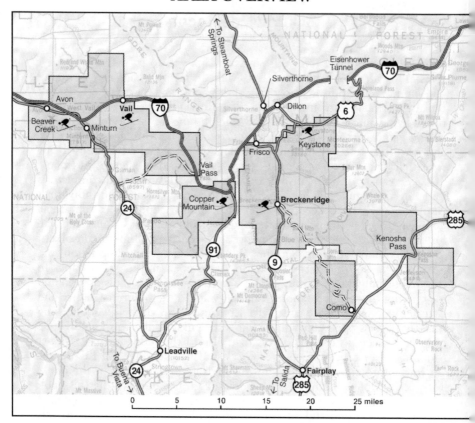

TABLE OF CONTENTS

TABLE OF CONTENTS

WELCOME TO THE GREAT MOUNTAIN BIKING IN BRECKENRIDGE, KEYSTONE, COPPER MOUNTAIN AND VAIL!

These mountain towns offer uncrowded trails with wonderful views, lots of fresh air and cool mountain breezes, and plenty of wildflowers in the summer and colorful aspens in the fall. There are trails for every level of mountain biker, including lift access downhilling for beginner to expert riders. This book is written for folks who want to experience the great singletrack rides around Summit County and Vail. It fits right in your pack for easy reference out on the trail. Please read the trail descriptions in full to help you decide on a ride that fits your ability, desires, and time schedule. Take along at least one of the maps mentioned for the ride, as they offer a much larger overview and all connecting routes. Please read this entire introduction as well, so you understand the descriptions and are prepared for each ride.

A few considerations before heading out on the rides:

High altitude: The towns of Breckenridge and Vail are at the altitudes of 9602 and 8100 feet, respectively, and many of the rides climb above 10,000 and even up to 12,000 feet or more. Before attempting the higher and more strenuous rides, plan on spending a few days here riding shorter rides and taking it easy if you are from a lower altitude or not accustomed to mountain biking on a regular basis. Many of the lower and easier grade rides offer great singletrack and nice views, as well. Drink extra water before, during and after rides. Be sure to eat well and get extra nutrients and electrolytes in your diet. Know your limits and respect them, too! If you aren't feeling well, it could be the altitude. Take the day off and rest, and see a doctor if needed.

Weather: Storms can blow in quickly in the mountains, so check the weather before starting your day and plan a ride accordingly. Get started as early as possible, so you can be off the high ridges and peaks when afternoon thunderstorms roll through, as they often do, even when the day starts out clear. If the weather looks threatening, ride near town and stay at lower altitude. Save that epic ride for a clear day! Be prepared with warm clothes and raingear, and plan exits from long rides in case the weather turns stormy.

Route Finding: There are many junctions and spur roads and trails, and a lack of signs in Summit County and Vail. Take this guide, one or more accurate maps, and a compass with you to help you find your way. Each description tells you which map or maps are best for the individual ride. Know how to read the map and use the compass. Keep track of surrounding landmarks. Work your way up to the longer and more primitive rides as you get to know the area and its' landmarks. Always stay on the marked trails, the terrain is rugged and you could get in worse trouble by bushwhacking. Hire a local guide if you are afraid of getting lost.

Trail Conditions: Check with a local bike shop (see listing in the back of this book) for current trail conditions before setting out on rides. In the spring many of the trails don't melt out until well into June or even into July. After rainstorms, many of the trails stay wet and slick for up to several days. Don't ride muddy trails, and walk around muddy sections. Riding muddy trails speeds erosion, and it generally isn't all that fun to push your bike through the mud. A big snowstorm in the fall can close trails at higher altitude earlier than usual or suggested in the description. Many trails have stream crossings, be sure to check with the bike shop to see if they are safe to cross if you are riding the trail in the spring or early summer.

Clothing and gear: Good gear can make your day! Make sure you always carry a jacket even on the shortest rides. It can cool off quickly here in the mountains, and high view points where you want to take a break are often breezy and cool. On all day rides and cooler days, bring leggings or tights, a warm fleece or polypro shirt, a good waterproof or gore-tex type jacket, and full finger gloves. Gore-tex pants are a good idea to bring as well, as the temperature can drop 20 degrees if a storm rolls in. Being caught in a severe rain or snow storm is not unusual even in the summer months. Always wear a good fitting helmet! Camelbak-type packs are the best for carrying enough water and all your gear and food. On epic rides or long rides in unfamiliar areas, throw in a headlamp and a warm headband that fits under your helmet. Bring a basic first-aid kit, as well.

Water and food: Always take extra water and food! Even on the shortest rides in this book, take a snack and a water bottle. On epic rides take a full 100 oz. camelback, two full waterbottles and a pack full of high energy food: sandwiches, fruit, nuts, etc. Sugary foods are not enough for longer rides. Drink extra water at high altitude, and eat often to retain your energy. A water filter is a good addition to your pack, and is lighter weight than extra water bottles. Check your maps and get local bike shop advice to make sure there are year round streams on the epic ride you have planned. It is not a good idea to drink unfiltered stream water, as it is possible to get giardia and similar digestive ailments from it.

Tools: Always take along basic tools and know how to use them. It's a long walk home, even from the shortest rides. Carry a good pump, an extra tube, a patchkit, a tire patch, allen wrenches, a chain tool, lube, and a rag and stiff brush to clean up your chain if it gets dry or muddy. Also bring a lighter in case of the unfortunate event of getting lost and needing to build a fire.

Maintainence: Keep your bike in good running order at all times! Check it over before every ride to make sure everything is tight and in good shape. Keep your chain clean and lubed. If you don't know how to do this, take it to a shop regularly. Get a good book or take a clinic and learn to be prepared to perform trailside repairs.

Maps: Many of the rides are not well marked and there may be many junctions and spurs along the routes. Bring this book along to help you find your way. The maps in this book may not be exact to scale, so also bring a more detailed and up-to-date map or maps for the area on each ride. The best for the area are The Latitude 40 Summit County Colorado Trails Map and The Sky Terrain Summit, Vail and Holy Cross Map. Both are new in 2004.

A Few Tips for Riding:

Stay in control at all times to avoid an injury to yourself or others, or a serious mechanical. Some of the rides are quite isolated, and you may not see another person if you need help. Stay with the marked trails if you do end up walking back. Always carry a map. The destination of important spurs along the routes are described in the individual trail descriptions in the event of such an emergency. Don't follow a spur unless you know where it leads, as you could get lost. Keep in mind that there are new user created trails every year, so not all roads and trails are on the maps in this book or any larger map.

Introduction

Respect private property, trail closures, and wilderness areas, and stay on existing roads and trails. Sections of many trails travel across private property, respect the owners by staying on the trail and passing quietly. Respect no trespassing signs. Close all gates behind you. Don't ride in wilderness areas, it is illegal and carries a heavy fine. If you are caught, your bike may be confiscated. Most trails in wilderness are too rough or steep to ride anyway. Don't ride closed trails. It is against the White River Travel Plan to ride off trail or create new ones, and carries a heavy fine. Responsible use helps keep our trails open! Do not enter or explore any of the open mine shafts, pits or old structures when riding around Summit County's mining areas. Many of these are dangerous and most are private property as well.

Respect other users and create a feeling of peace out on the trails. Always yield the right of way to horses and other animals. Don't ride quickly up on horses, let them know you are coming and ask permission to walk past, or dismount to let them pass if they are coming toward you. Don't chase or spook livestock or wildlife. Let them get off the trail before passing. I know of a chased cow that doubled back and ran over a rider in the group after being chased by the lead rider! Luckily the rider escaped with only a ruined rim. Always yield the right of way to hikers, and to motorcyclists as well. If they drive off the trail to go around you, soon we'll only have doubletracks. Watch out for small animals and birds, they tend to be hard to see until the last minute. Keep your speed down in tall vegetation to avoid running them over. Pack out your trash and leave no trace that you've been there. Don't squash vegetation with your bike or yourself.

Ride the bike path or dirt roads instead of driving to trails and trailheads, when possible. Many of the trails start very close to town and it is simple to ride right from your lodging. A road warm-up is great for getting in shape and improves your riding ability on the trail. It is more environmentally friendly than driving. If you do drive to a trailhead, slow down and pass other riders and hikers slowly. The bus system in Summit County will haul your bike for free. For more information, call the Summit stage at 970-668-0999, or pick up a map for the bus at the Breckenridge Information Center at 309 Main Street, or call 970-453-6018. The paved bike path systems in both Summit County and Vail lead to many of the trailheads for a safe ride to or from most trails.

Protect yourself during hunting season (mid-September through November) by wearing hunter orange and staying on popular trails. Find out from the Forest Service where most hunters will be during your stay.

Disclaimer:

Finally, I will assume you know: how to ride your bike, your limits and when to turn back, basic navigation and route finding, basic bike repairs, and what to do in case of an emergency. This book is simply a trail guide, intended to help you pick out and find rides. It is not meant to replace basic knowledge of mountain biking and backcountry travel, maps, navigation skills, or just plain common sense. Inaccuracies may be present within the ride descriptions, always double check the information with other accurate resources including USGS and other detailed maps, and trail signs. The author, the producer, the designers, and the publisher of this book, and anyone mentioned in or associated with this book are in no way responsible or liable for anyone using this book and the suggested routes within this book. Mountain biking is a hazardous sport with unforeseen risks and dangers, including but not limited to: getting lost, injured, heat stroke, hypothermia, and even death. Cyclists must assume responsibility for themselves. Be careful out there, be responsible, and have fun!

How to use this book

Each ride description begins with an overview of the important statistics for the ride so you can decide which rides suit your abilities and skill level. Here is an explanation of all the elements of the descriptions.

Description: A short, general overview of the ride.

Distance: As close as possible in tenths of miles, and also a breakdown of singletrack, dirt road, and paved road in miles. Please note that due to differences in maps, computers, weather, etc., that the distances might be slightly different than what your computer reads. I have described important points in the trail with landmarks as well as mileage to help you find the routes even if you don't ride with a computer. Use maps, a compass, trail signs, landmarks, and this guide to help you be sure of your location.

Time: A general guide for the time it will take to complete the ride, including short rest breaks. The time listed is a range for the level of rider that matches the rides' difficulty rating, or a rider of a higher level of expertise. If a ride is listed as an expert ride, the time range is for expert riders. If the ride is listed as intermediate, the fastest time would apply to an expert rider and the longer time would apply to an intermediate rider, and so on. Ride times can vary greatly from this range due to weather, trail conditions, mechanicals, long rest breaks, or a rider's physical condition and ability, to name a few factors. Read into the description and make appropriate time allowance based on your knowledge of your own level of riding and experience. Always allow extra time for a ride!

Difficulty: A general rating. Read entire individual descriptions to get a better idea of how tough the rides are. Distance, steepness and length of climbs, and the amount and degree of difficulty of technical obstacles, as well as the difficulty following the trails are considered in the rating. Beginner rides are for those with little experience mountain biking. Intermediate riders are assumed to have ridden moderate singletrack many times and be fairly comfortable on it, be in fairly good physical condition, and have a good knowledge of how to handle their bike in moderately technical situations. Intermediate rides can also be as long as 20 miles. Advanced intermediate is a step up, involving longer trails and more singletrack and technical riding. Strong advanced intermediate riders would probably do fine on several of the expert rides, however, I suggest starting with intermediate rides to gauge the difficulty ratings before setting out on expert rides. The expert rating is for experienced riders who can handle several hours in the saddle and very technical trails. Some rides rated expert may not be so long, but have a lot of challenging technical riding involved, or visa-versa. Epic rides are for strong expert riders only. They are very long, rough, and sometimes difficult to follow. These rides challenge the strongest of riders with long climbs at high altitude and continuous technical singletrack, and also the rider's ability to navigate when the trail becomes braided or disappears. They are for the adventurous rider who can truly ride all day, and doesn't mind carrying their bike.

Introduction

Technical skill: The Beginner rating has little in the way of technical obstacles, the Intermediate rating has a moderate amount of technical obstacles or shorter distances of them, the Expert rating may have very difficult obstacles and/or long distances of technical riding. Technical obstacles include rocks and rocky sections, deadfall, exposed tree roots on the trail which can be even more tricky when wet, exposure where a fall could send a rider down a steep bank or cliff, creek crossings, boggy areas, etc.

Aerobic effort: Whether the ride demands easy, moderate, high, or strenuous aerobic output. If you are from a lower altitude, a ride may seem more difficult to you than the aerobic rating given. Many rides in Summit County and Vail challenge even experienced riders because of the altitude. If you are concerned about the difficulty of the ride, start by riding shorter, easier rides first, and allowing extra time for the ride.

Elevation: Top: The highest elevation of the ride, in feet. Gain: The approximate gain in elevation for the ride, in feet.

Season: This is a general guide to when the ride is free of snow and dry. Please visit a local bike shop to find out if trails are in good condition and dry before riding them, regardless of the time of year. Snow can keep trails closed later in the spring than usual, or close them with an early fall storm, before expected. Heavy or prolonged periods of rain common to the mountains can affect trail conditions for several days. Please don't ride muddy trails, it speeds erosion and makes them bumpy when they dry.

Usage: How heavily the trail is used: Light, moderate, heavy.

Finding route: Easy, moderate, or difficult. This rating assumes you carry this book and one of the maps I suggest in the ride description, and have a good knowledge of route finding. This rating is based on the clarity of the trails, the amount of turns on a ride, and how well marked it is.

Maps: The map or maps that best illustrate the ride.

Mileage log: Measured with an accurate cylcocomputer. These points could be slightly off for various reasons, so I have included descriptions of landmarks along the routes to help you decipher where you are if you don't have a computer on your bike or if your numbers don't match the description exactly. Some of the mile points have (approx. mileage) after them, this is to alert you to a possible greater difference. Again use several resources to be sure of where you are.

Options: Options to extend or shorten rides or try other routes. At the end of mileage log. 🚲

MAP LEGEND

══════════	Highways
══════════	Paved Roads
:======	Dirt Roads (2WD driveable)
▬▬▬▬▬▬	Bike Paths
─ ─ ─ ─ ─ ─	Doubletrack / Jeep Road
─ ·· ─ ·· ─ ·· ─	Old Doubletrack (Non-Motorized)
···················	Singletrack
── · ── · ── · ──	Chairlifts
🆃🅷	Trailheads
🅿	Parking
■	Buildings
🎿	Ski Area
FS, FSR	Forest Service Road
CR	County Road

The Summit Fat Tire Society is a non-profit organization dedicated to the preservation of Mountain Biking in Summit County. The SFTS works with land managers and private land owners to maintain and create trails and to preserve access. The SFTS also works to educate mountain bikers in environnmentally sound riding practices. These folks host many trail maintenance projects and social rides throughout the year. Visit their website www.sfts.us to find out more information and get involved!

THE FLUME TRAILS

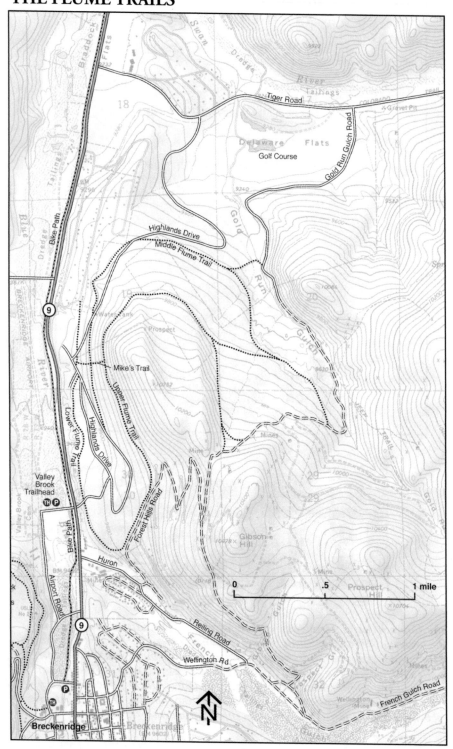

Description:

The Flume Trails are short, smooth singletrack trails through dense conifer forest near Breckenridge. They are easily accessed by the paved bike path from Breckenridge. The trails are perfect for a quick afternoon loop or as a connector to rides in the Swan River drainage, see option 2. These trails pass through a lot of private property, please respect these folks by staying on the trail! Here I describe one possible intermediate loop connecting most of the trails, or see option 1 below for a short out and back beginner ride.

Distance: 6.7 miles, .5 mile of pavement, 6.2 miles of singletrack.

Time: 1-1 ½ hours.

Overall Difficulty: Intermediate, option 1 is beginner

Technical Skill: Beginner to Intermediate

Aerobic Effort: Low to Moderate

Elevation: Top: 9,920' Gain: 450'

Season: June through October

Usage: Moderate

Finding Route: Easy to moderate. Well marked and easy to follow down low. This loop connects several short sections of trail that cross The Highlands subdivision roads. The continuation is usually directly across the road it crosses, and riders may not need to stop and look at the directions for many of the crossings. Up higher there are several unmarked turns.

Location: From French Street on the north end of Breckenridge, drive north 7/10ths of a mile on Highway 9 to Valley Brook Road, turn left and cross the Blue River. On the right is a large parking lot and the Valley Brook Trailhead. If you ride from town, take the paved bike path from Watson Avenue directly to the trailhead. There is a large public parking lot south of Watson Avenue.

Maps: Latitude 40 Summit County Colorado Trails

Mileage Log:

0.0 Ride out of the parking lot, and turn left on Valley Brook Drive. Ride straight across Highway 9 and up Highlands Road.

0.3 The signed Lower Flume Trail crosses the road at the top of the hill. Turn left and enjoy the smooth roll through the woods.

0.7 Stay to the right and climb, passing a faint spur.

0.9 Intersect Barney Ford Circle and Highlands Drive. Turn left and ride down Highlands Drive 1/10th of a mile.

1.0 Turn right on the continuation of The Lower Flume, and take an immediate right on Mike's Trail when the trail forks. Climb steeply for 1/10th of a mile.

1.1 Turn left on the signed Middle Flume Trail. This section is smooth and rolling.

3.3	Cross a road, riding straight ahead and onto a private drive, then immediately turn right onto the continuation of the Middle Flume.
1.7	Ride straight ahead, crossing Spalding Terrace.
1.8	Ride straight ahead and cross Highlands Road.
2.5	Cross Preston Way, the trail continues straight ahead. Climb steadily.
3.1	Turn right at an unmarked intersection. (Left leads to Gold Run Gulch Road, see option 2, below.)
3.3	Stay right at an unmarked intersection and begin descending.
3.7	Turn left over a bridge.
3.9	Cross Golden Age Drive and roll onto the Upper Flume. This is fast fun!
4.2	Stay left, passing Mike's Trail on the right.
5.6	Stay right with the trail and down a switchback. Forest Hills Road is on the left.
5.8	Arrive at the intersection of Upper and Lower Flume, turn right on the Lower Flume. This section is rocky and climbs.
6.3	Back to the beginning of the singletrack loop on Highlands Road. Turn left and ride down to the light.
6.6	Cross Highway 9.
6.7	Back to the parking lot.

Option 1: For a short beginner out and back ride, start as in the above loop and turn left on the Lower Flume Trail at mile 0.3. Ride for one mile or as far as you are comfortable with, and then turn back, retracing your tracks back to the parking lot. At mile 1.0, beginners can stay left and ride to the end of the Lower Flume and back, skipping the steep section of Mike's Trail.

Option 2: To use this trail to connect to Gold Run Gulch Road 300, turn left at mile 3.1. Stay left at mile points 3.2 and 3.4, passing spur dirt roads that head to the right and up. Intersect Gold Run Gulch Road at 3.7 miles. From here, turn left and ride down to Tiger Road. Turn right on Tiger Road to access the Horseshoe Gulch trail system at the Dredgeboat Trailhead, or the Colorado Trail farther up Tiger Road. See the Latitude 40 Summit County Colorado Trails Map for details. 🚲

Boreas Pass Road

BAKERS TANK • BARNEY FORD • BLUE RIVER • ARGENTINE TRAILS

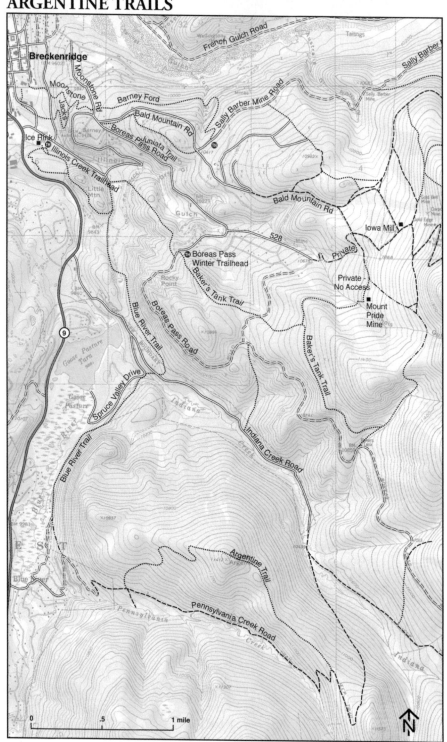

Description:

The Bakers Tank loop is a short non-motorized trail, starting 3 1/2 miles from Breckenridge. The loop begins with a smooth and gentle warm-up on Boreas Pass Road, located on the original Denver, South Park, and Pacific narrow gauge railroad route to Breckenridge. Boreas Pass Road offers wonderful views and cuts across steep aspen hillsides, making it a nice choice for an autumn color ride. Expect to see vehicle traffic on the narrow road, and other users on this popular trail. An easy section of trail follows, and leads into the dense conifer forest. A challenging singletrack descent finishes off the loop. The ride is also fun ridden in the opposite direction. If the gate past the trailhead is closed in the spring, the road is not yet dry. The trail takes longer than the road to dry out due to the dark forest it winds through. To ride the loop from town, park at the Illinois Creek Trailhead, see Location and option 1, below. For a singletrack option to take back down, see option 2. The Boreas Pass Road offers a few dispersed camping options.

Distance: 6 mile loop from the Boreas Pass Winter Trailhead, 3 miles of dirt road and 3 miles of singletrack. Ridden from town add 7 miles of paved road and/or singletrack.

Time: 1-1 ½ hours from the trailhead, 2-2 ½ hours from town.

Overall Difficulty: Advanced intermediate

Technical Skill: Advanced intermediate

Aerobic Effort: Moderate

Elevation: Top: 10,850' Gain: 600', add 760 feet if ridden from town.

Season: Late June through October

Usage: Heavy

Finding Route: Easy

Location: Drive south on Breckenridge's Main Street (Highway 9) and turn left at the last stoplight onto Boreas Pass Road. Drive 3.5 miles up to the Winter Trailhead and park here. To ride up, drive 1/4 mile on Boreas Pass Road and turn right into the far end of the ice rink parking lot. Park here at the Illinois Creek Trailhead. Ride Boreas Pass Road to the trailhead, or for singletrack, see option 1.

Maps: Latitude 40 Summit County Colorado Trails map or the Sky Terrain for Summit, Vail and Holy Cross

Mileage Log:

0.0 Begin (or continue) riding up Boreas Pass Road from the Winter Trailhead.

1.5 Continue on Boreas Pass Road, passing trail access on the left.

1.6 Pass an unmarked singletrack on the right. This leads down to Indiana Creek Road.

3.0 Turn left just before the Bakers Tank. Climb up to the trail entrance.

3.1 Ride through the pole fence and onto the signed Bakers Tank Trail. The trail forks immediately, turn left.

BAKERS TANK TRAIL
Ride Information

3.3   Lookout and good lunch spot on the left.

4.0   Turn left and descend at the fork. Right leads to private property. No access here.

4.9   Merge with a doubletrack that comes in from the right, then cross another doubletrack. Swing right and then left onto the singletrack. Follow the blue diamonds that mark the trail.

6.0   End at the Winter Trailhead.

Option 1: To ride to the trailhead from town on challenging singletrack: Cross Boreas Pass Road from the Illinois Creek Trailhead to Sunbeam Road. Take this 1/10th to access Jacks Cruel Joke on the right. Take Jack's up and then turn left in 3/10th of a mile onto the Hermit Placer Trail. Continue on this flume trail for 4/10th of a mile, take two rights, and begin climbing the signed Moonstone Trail. When you intersect Moonstone Road in 6/10th of a mile, turn right and ride 1/10th of a mile to Boreas Pass Road, then turn left and ride 1 ½ miles to the trailhead.

Option 2: To descend to town on singletrack: After completing the Bakers Tank loop, turn left at the winter trailhead on Boreas Pass Road.

6.1   Just after crossing the Forest Boundary, take the unmarked singletrack to your right. This turn is less than 1/10th of a mile from where the Bakers Tank Trail ends. Stay left and below a few homes.

6.3   The trail levels and rolls through an aspen grove.

6.5   Stay left, passing a mine.

6.7   The trail forks. Stay left to avoid the steep drop-off and mine tailings.

6.8   Cross the drive at Wakefield's and ride onto the marked Blue River Trail. (Or turn right to intersect Boreas Pass Road and left to reach your vehicle.)

7.0   Turn right and climb the hill at the fork next to the fence.

7.2   Stay on the most obvious and easiest grade trail through this braided section. Pass doubletracks that spur off to the right and left.

7.7   Stay right and descend.

7.8   Turn right and ride to the Illinois Creek Trailhead. 🚲

BARNEY FORD TO BAKERS TANK JUNIATA TRAIL
Ride Information ———————————— *See map page 14*

Description:

This Breckenridge loop combines several trails and roads for a mostly singletrack loop that starts right in town. Enjoy great views from up high on Bald Mountain, and fast singletrack descents. Many more roads and singletracks invite exploration once you become familiar with the area. For a shorter loop on the Juniata Trail, see option 3, below.

Distance: 12 mile loop, 2.5 miles of dirt road, 2 miles of paved road, 7.5 miles of singletrack. See option 1 for more singletrack and less road!

Time: 2- 2 ½ hours

Overall Difficulty: Advanced Intermediate

Technical Skill: Advanced Intermediate with an expert section on the descent.

Aerobic Effort: Moderate

Elevation: Top: 11,680' Gain: 2,200'

Season: Mid-June through October

Usage: Moderate

Finding Route: Moderate to Difficult. This loop links several trails and roads, many of which are not marked. The lower trails in the beginning and the end of the loop are easy to follow, but near the Bald Mountain Road and above, it is easy to get turned around on the maze of roads and trails. You will need to pay close attention to directions.

Location: Drive or ride south on Breckenridge's Main Street (Highway 9) and turn left at the last stoplight onto Boreas Pass Road. Continue 1/4 mile and turn right into the far end of the ice rink parking lot. Park here at the Illinois Creek Trailhead.

Maps: Latitude 40 Summit County Colorado Trails AND Sky Terrain Summit, Vail and Holy Cross. Neither is 100% accurate for the Bald Mountain Area, but both together are very useful.

Mileage Log:

0.0   Begin riding up Boreas Pass Road. (See option 1 for a singletrack option.)

1.7   Turn left onto Moonstone Road. This is located just before Bald Mountain Road. Ride down Moonstone Road less than 1/10th mile and turn right on the signed Barney Ford Trail. Barney Ford climbs via a series of gradual switchbacks.

3.3   End the Barney Ford Trail at a paved trailhead on Sally Barber Road. Turn left and start riding on the dirt continuation of Sally Barber Road.

3.7   Turn right onto the singletrack. This is just before a pole fence, and there are brown signs stating private property ahead, follow the signed trail.

3.9   Ride onto a paved private road. Turn left and follow to the cul-de-sac where the continuation of the trail goes right and up.

4.5   Stay left passing a spur road to the right. The trail narrows to a singletrack.

4.7   The singletrack forks, turn right.

4.8   Turn right on an old narrow doubletrack when the singletrack ends.

BARNEY FORD TO BAKERS TANK JUNIATA TRAIL
Ride Information

4.9 Turn left at the end of the spur road on Bald Mountain Road. Climb on this prominent rocky road, passing another spur road on the left, until you reach the Iowa Mill. This is a large metal building with "Iowa Mill" on the front. It is a good landmark in this maze of roads and trails.

5.5 Reach the Iowa Mill at the unmarked junction of Bald Mountain Road and Forest Road 586. Turn left and climb.

5.6 Stay right and pass an old doubletrack spur to the left on a switchback, and continue climbing.

5.9 At the corner of the next switchback, turn right off Bald Mountain Road onto an old doubletrack spur. Climb up a little and pass some mining debris.

6.2 Stay on the main road here as you descend briefly and traverse above the powerlines.

6.3 Pass a steep road cutoff to the right, then almost immediately the road forks. Stay left and continue traversing under Bald Mountain.

6.5 Pass an old cabin below on the right.

6.8 Top out under the powerlines. The road narrows to singletrack. Begin a steep and eroded but fun downhill, switchbacking down under the powerlines.

7.1 Stay right, don't cross Tank Creek.

7.4 Stay right, don't cross Tank Creek.

7.5 Arrive at a fork. Turn right and continue on the Bakers Tank singletrack. (Or see option 2 below for other singletrack options.)

8.4 The trail forks, continue left and begin descending. Right leads to private property, no access allowed.

9.3 Merge with a doubletrack that comes in from the right, then cross another doubletrack. Swing right and then left onto the continuation of the singletrack. Stay with the obvious route and follow the blue diamonds that mark this trail.

10.4 End at the Boreas Pass Winter Trailhead. Turn left here and cross the forest boundary and seasonal closure gate, and take the unsigned singletrack to the right. Stay left below a couple of houses.

10.7 The trail levels and rolls through an aspen grove.

10.8 Stay left, passing a mine.

11.0 Turn left at the trail fork to avoid a steep drop-off from the mine tailings.

11.1 Arrive at the Wakefields Ranch. Cross the drive and ride onto the marked continuation of the Blue River Trail that follows the fence. (Or turn right to intersect Boreas Pass Road, turn left and ride back to your vehicle.)

11.3 Turn right and at the fork next to the fence, and climb up over the hill.

11.5 Descend on the most used and easiest grade trail through this braided section. Pass doubletracks that spur off to left and right.

12.0 Stay right and descend.

12.1 Turn right and head back to the Illinois Creek Trailhead.

Option 1: To ride a challenging singletrack up, take Jack's Cruel Joke, Hermit Placer and Moonstone Trails: From the Illinois Creek Trailhead parking area, cross Boreas Pass Road and continue 1/10th mile on Sunbeam Road to the signed Jack Cruel Joke. Turn right and climb 3/10th mile and take a sharp left onto the Hermit Placer Trail. Ride 4/10th mile and turn right and immediately right again onto the Moonstone Trail. Climb this challenging tight trail 6/10th mile to Moonstone Road. Cross and begin the Barney Ford Trail (mile point 1.7 above.) This is about ½ mile shorter than taking the road.

Option 2: For a different singletrack descent from mile 7.5 above, continue down to Boreas Pass Road and turn left. Ride about one mile to an unmarked singletrack on the right. This trail starts directly across from a cutback road to the left that leads up to a camp spot, the first spur you will come to. (The mileage is approximate, please look for the spur road. If you come to a major spur in Boreas Pass Road, you have gone too far.) Descend on this singletrack to Indiana Creek Road. Turn right and ride until you see the signed Blue River Trail and follow this back to Wakefield's. Turn left and up over the hill to the parking lot at the Illinois Creek Trailhead, or straight back to Boreas Pass Road. Another option would be to ride the Bakers Tank Trail from mile 7.5 until mile 9.3 above, and turn left on the doubletrack. This leads you back to Boreas Pass Road. Turn left here and immediately begin looking for a singletrack that leads off to the right, just past a big group of willows in the drainage. This also leads to Indiana Creek Road, and is a bit longer. Refer to the Latitude 40 Summit County Colorado map for details on these explorations.

Option 3: To ride the Juniata Trail back to Breckenridge, ride to mile 3.3, above. Turn right on the paved section of Sally Barber Road. 3.5 Turn right on Bald Mountain Road, and immediately left on the Juniata Trail, just before Juniata Circle. 4.0 Continue straight ahead. 4.1 Turn left over bridge. 4.4 Cross Bald Mountain Road. 4.5 Cross Moonstone Road and continue on the Moonstone Trail. 5.1 Turn left and then immediately left again, on Hermit Placer.5.5 Turn sharp right on Jack's Cruel Joke. 5.8 Turn left on Sunbeam Road to return to the Illinois Creek Trailhead. 6.0 Back to your vehicle. 🚲

BLUE RIVER TRAIL

See map page 14 ————————————— #### Ride Information

Description:

This smooth, non-motorized singletrack ride starts right in Breckenridge. It winds through the dark woods and quaking aspens, and follows an old ditch bank where riders can enjoy nice views of The Goose Pasture Tarn and Ten Mile Range. It is an easy afternoon ride. It is also a good connector to longer loops like the Argentine Trail on the east of Highway 9 (see Blue River to Argentine Trail, page 21) and the Spruce Creek, Burro, and Wheeler Trails on the west side. Ridden as an out and back, enjoy a great descent back to town. This trail travels through private property, please stay on the trail and respect the access.

Distance: 7.2 miles out and back, all singletrack!

Time: 1-1 ½ hours

Overall Difficulty: Easy Intermediate

Technical Skill: Easy Intermediate.

Aerobic Effort: Moderate

Elevation: Top: 10,150' Gain: 800'

Season: June through October

Usage: Moderate

Finding Route: Easy

Location: Drive or ride south on Breckenridge's Main Street (Highway 9) and turn left at the last stoplight onto Boreas Pass Road. Continue 1/4 mile and turn right into the far end of the ice rink parking lot. Park here at the Illinois Creek Trailhead.

Maps: Latitude 40 Summit County Colorado Trails or Sky Terrain Summit, Vail and Holy Cross map.

Mileage Log:

0.0 Leave the parking lot and turn right onto Boreas Pass Road.

0.6 Turn right off the first switchback into a driveway. Ride toward the large "Wakefield" signed gate.

0.7 Turn right at the gate onto the marked Blue River Trail singletrack and ride along the fence.

0.8 Ride straight ahead, passing a couple forks to the right. (These head back to the Illinois Creek Trailhead.) Climb for ¼ mile, then roll along this smooth wooded section.

2.1 Descend to the paved Indiana Creek Road. Turn right and ride down the road very briefly, and turn left on the signed continuation of the Blue River Trail.

2.3 Arrive at another paved road. Turn left and cross the creek. The trail continues left on the same side of the road. Climb gradually.

2.4 Arrive at a signed intersection on private property. Ride straight ahead over an old doubletrack and up a hill.

2.9 Views of the Goose Pasture Tarn and Ten Mile Range.

3.6 Arrive at a dirt street across from some houses. Turn around and return the way you came.

7.2 Back at the Illinois Creek Trailhead.

Option: For a different and more challenging way back, turn left on the singletrack next to the Wakefield's fence at mile 6.4. Follow this up over the hill.

6.6 Ride straight down the most used trail through this braided section, passing spur doubletracks on the right and left. Follow this along above Highway 9.

7.1 Stay right and descend.

7.2 Turn right at the fork and ride back to the parking lot. 🚲

BLUE RIVER AND ARGENTINE TRAILS
See map page 14 ————————————— **Ride Information**

Description:

This loop starts right in Breckenridge and links the easy Blue River Trail with the more advanced Argentine Mountain Trail via beautiful Pennsylvania Creek Road. Most of Pennsylvania Creek Road is a gradual spin through creek-side meadows. After winding up a densely forested ridge, the Argentine Trail offers awesome views of Bald and Boreas Mountains, and The Ten Mile and Mosquito Ranges. A challenging and fun switch-backing descent finishes off the keyhole loop before returning back to Breckenridge the way you came. The Argentine Trail is used by motorcycles so keep an eye out for them. The Argentine Trail would be difficult in reverse because of the steep, loose climb.

Distance: 14.5 mile keyhole loop, 6.5 miles of doubletrack, 8 miles of singletrack.

Time: 2 1/2-3 hours

Overall Difficulty: Expert

Technical Skill: Expert

Aerobic Effort: Moderately high

Elevation: Top: 11,412' Gain: 2,460'

Season: mid-June to October

Usage: Light

Finding Route: Mostly Easy, some intersections are not marked.

Location: Drive or ride south on Breckenridge's Main Street (Highway 9) and turn left at the last stoplight onto Boreas Pass Road. Continue 1/4 mile and turn right into the far end of the ice rink parking lot. Park here at the Illinois Creek Trailhead.

Maps: Latitude 40 Summit County Colorado Trails is the best for this ride, or Sky Terrain Summit, Vail, and Holy Cross

Mileage Log:

0.0 Ride south out of the parking lot onto a singletrack behind the Illinois

Creek Trailhead sign, and over a bridge. Turn immediately left on the Illinois Creek Loop High at the signed intersection. (If you prefer a more gradual warm-up, see The Blue River Trail, page 19, and follow the directions to 0.8.)

0.1 Stay left and high, then at the fork turn left toward the Blue River Pathway.

0.5 Stay right on the easiest and most used trail as the route becomes braided.

0.6 Pass signed spur roads to the left and right.

0.8 Descend to a fence and Wakefield's Ranch. Turn right. Climb for ¼ mile then roll along this smooth, beautiful trail.

2.1 Descend to the paved Indiana Creek Road. Turn right and descend the road briefly, and turn left on the signed Blue River Trail.

2.3 Turn left on the paved Spruce Valley Road, and cross the creek. The trail continues on the same side of the road. Climb gradually.

2.4 Ride straight ahead over an old doubletrack and up a hill.

2.9 Views of the Goose Pasture Tarn and the Ten Mile Range.

3.6 Arrive at a dirt street. Turn left here and immediately left onto an unmarked, steep and rocky dirt road.

4.0 Turn left and climb the gravel Pennsylvania Creek Road. After a few steep switchbacks, the road climbs more gradually alongside the creek.

5.0 Ride straight ahead, passing a spur that forks to the right.

5.1 Ride straight on the main road as the wide Argentine Trail comes in on the left and a spur road heads off to the right.

6.4 Trail 611 turns right off the first switchback. Stay left and continue climbing on the road, more steeply now.

6.8 On the fourth switchback turn left onto the unmarked Argentine Mountain Trail. The singletrack starts out flat and then rolls along the top of the ridge, climbing gradually. A few stingers challenge your climbing skills. Heavy motorcycle use has left steeper sections rutted and loose.

8.1 Arrive at the high point, 11,412 feet. Nice views of Bald and Boreas Mountains to the east, Red Mountain and Red Peak to the south, and the Mosquitos and The Ten Mile Range to the south and west. Begin a fast descent.

9.5 Back to the Pennsylvania Creek Road. Turn right and ride downhill to return the way you came.

14.5 Back to the trailhead.

Option: At mile 10.4, if you haven't had enough, continue down Pennsylvania Creek Road to Highway 9 and turn right. Ride Carefully along the shoulder to Spruce Creek Road and turn left. Climb this road about two miles to the Burro Trail and follow this to the Breckenridge Ski Area. Another option off Spruce Creek Road is to turn left onto the Wheeler Trail (9/10ths of a mile past the Burro Trail) and follow this to McCullough Gulch and back. 🚲

The Wheeler Trail

BRECKENRIDGE SKI AREA

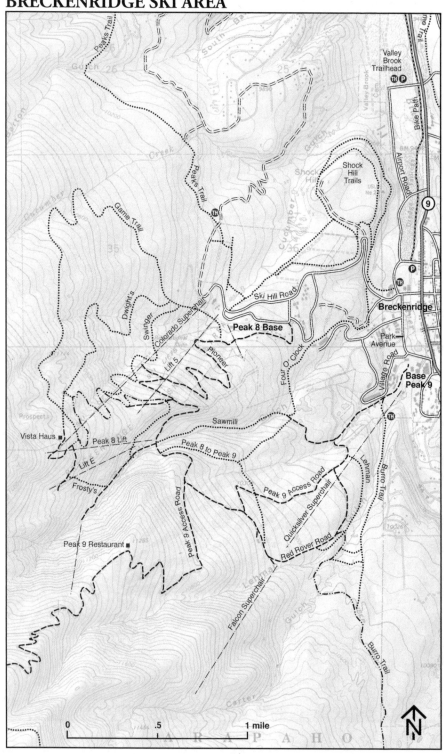

BRECKENRIDGE SKI AREA
Ride Information

The Breckenridge Ski Area has several fun cross country mountain biking trails that can be linked in a variety of ways, or ridden downhill only with the use of a daily lift ticket and bike haul. Maps and tickets are available at the ticket office at the Peak 8 Base Area, two miles up Ski Hill Road. These uncrowded trails are mostly moderate, with only a few difficult sections. They are well marked during the summer season. These bike trails are especially quiet after the summer season (early June to Labor Day) is over and the lifts are not running. Uphill riding is allowed on all the trails. There are great views of the surrounding mountains from the rides. The only drawback of these trails is that they stick near the runs and lifts. Don't miss the 4 O'clock Free Ride Park, with obstacles to test everyone's skills. It is located off the 4 O'clock Road and trail. ᘘ

BRECKENRIDGE SKI AREA
Loop 1: Pioneer Trail, Frosty's, Lehman, Peak 8 to Peak 9 and Swinger
Ride Information

Description:

The Pioneer Trail is a gradual, enjoyable way to access several of the rides on the Breckenridge Ski Area, winding up to high altitude views and ending at the Vista Haus. It is mostly singletrack and old doubletrack, so you won't see too much traffic on your ride. Descending Frosty's Challenge and Sawmill Creek, two short but fun advanced intermediate descents, is a blast. From here, riders can ride back to town on the 4 O'clock Trail, see option 2, or continue on for more singletrack fun. Climbing up the gradual Lehman and Peak 8 to Peak 9 Trails, and on to the Swinger Switchbacks descent ends the figure-8 loop back at the Peak 8 base area. With the Latitude 40 map, explore the Burro and Peaks Trail from the Breckenridge Ski Area.

Distance: 11.8 mile figure-8 loop, 3 miles of dirt road and 7.8 miles of singletrack. Add two miles if you ride up from town, see option 1.

Time: 2-2 ½ hours

Overall Difficulty: Advanced Intermediate

Technical Skill: Advanced Intermediate with a short section of expert descent.

Aerobic Effort: Moderate

Elevation: Top: 11,160'. Gain: 2,080'. Add 400 feet if you ride from town.

Season: June through October

Usage: Moderate

Finding Route: Easy to Moderate. The trails are well marked during the summer season, making the routes easy to follow. After the summer season, the signs are taken down, making route finding a little more challenging. The main routes are in most places obvious. It is hard to get truly lost from the ski area, usually you will end up at one base or the other.

Location: Begin at the Peak 8 Base, two miles up Ski Hill Road from the town of Breckenridge. To get here, either drive or ride up Ski Hill Road, or try

25

BRECKENRIDGE SKI AREA
Loop 1: Pioneer Trail, Frosty's, Lehman, Peak 8 to Peak 9 and Swinger
Ride Information

riding the Shock Hill Loops, see option 1.

Maps: Take along the Breckenridge Ski Area summer trails map, available at the Breckenridge Visitor Center and the ticket office at the Peak 8 Base Area; and the Latitude 40 Summit County Trails map.

Mileage Log:

0.0 Begin at the base of Lifts 7 and 5 at the bottom of the Peak 8 Base. The Pioneer Trail starts to the left of Lift 5 as you look up the mountain. The trail is fairly easy to follow even though it connects several sections of road and trail, follow the most obvious path.

0.2 Stay right with the singletrack. (There is a road on the left.)

0.5 Stay right with the singletrack.

0.7 Merge left onto the dirt road.

0.8 Turn left at the fork in the road.

0.9 Ride straight ahead as a steeper spur takes off left and up.

1.0 The road narrows to a wide singletrack again.

1.3 Stay right at a fork in the trail. Follow this long straightaway north.

1.6 Ride under a lift as the singletrack again becomes doubletrack, and climb gradually. The Swinger singletrack is below you on the next ski run.

1.8 Stay left with the road around a switchback, passing the Swinger singletrack off to the right.

2.0 Turn right off the road and onto a wide trail (an old road.) This turn is just before another ski run and an intersection with a major road. Continue on a long straightaway. Pass a "Powerline Run" ski sign here.

2.2 Stay left and continue climbing, passing the Swinger Trail.

2.4 Stay right on the singletrack just before the top of a lift, and climb a couple of rocky switchbacks.

2.6 Stay left on a switchback, passing Breakaway singletrack spur off to the right.

2.8 Cross a steep road, continue on singletrack.

2.9 The trail forks, stay right.

3.4 Stay left around the switchback, passing Klinko's singletrack to the right.

3.7 Stay left with the wide singletrack, passing a road on the right.

3.8 Arrive at an intersection under a chairlift. Turn left and descend on Frosty's Freeway Road. This is 1/10th of a mile before Vista Haus.

4.1 Just before reaching Lift 6 is a ski sign and Frosty's Challenge singletrack, turn left onto it and descend. This is a fun expert section.

4.8 Descend and turn left onto a dirt road below Lift G.

5.0 Continue on the road, passing a singletrack on the left.

5.3 Arrive at the bottom of the Peak 6 lift. Just to the left of and below the lift is the Sawmill Creek singletrack. Descend this fast and somewhat steep trail.

6.0 Arrive at the bottom of lift C. Turn right below the lift and follow the doubletrack. (Or you can exit here on the Four O'clock Trail. See option 2.)

6.1 Pass the Miners Trail on the right.

6.2 Stay on the road, passing a singletrack to the right, and descend to the Peak 9 access road.

6.3 Turn right on the access road and ride below the Peak 8 Super Connect lift. Climb to the next switchback.

6.4 Turn left on the Lehman Trail and ride straight across the lift line.

6.7 Climb to a fork and turn left. Dismount if you see horses in this area and let them pass.

6.9 Ride out of the woods and turn right at a fork, next to a small building. Ride toward the creek, cross a doubletrack and climb next to creek.

7.0 Cross a doubletrack. Continue on singletrack.

7.2 Turn left and ride uphill on a ski area access road. Pass the Falcon Superchair and a spur road on the left. Continue around the switchback.

7.5 Directly underneath the chairlift, turn right onto the Peak 8 to Peak 9 singletrack.

7.6 Traverse a ski run.

7.9 Cross an access road.

8.1 Pass the Miners Trail on the right, and cross an access road.

8.8 End of the singletrack. Turn right and ride down to the Peak 8 Lift. Turn left and climb up the road.

9.1 Turn right onto the contouring singletrack.

9.5 End on an access road. Turn right onto the road, then turn immediately left onto another road. Turn immediately left again and climb a switchback onto a wide singletrack straightaway. This is the Pioneer Trail.

9.7 Turn right onto the Swinger singletrack, out in a ski run, and begin descending gentle switchbacks.

10.1 Stay left with singletrack, and descend more steeply.

10.6 Cross a road.

10.9 Cross a road.

11.1 Stay right, passing a singletrack spur up to left. The trail widens to a doubletrack.

11.5 Stay right at a fork.

11.7 Back to the Peak 8 base area.

BRECKENRIDGE SKI AREA
Loop 1: Pioneer Trail, Frosty's, Lehman, Peak 8 to Peak 9 and Swinger
Ride Information

Option 1: To ride up to the Peak 8 Base Area on the Shock Hill Trails: Access these at the Watson Trailhead, off North Park Avenue and Ski Hill Road, across from the large public parking area. It is a bit confusing in this area because of the many trails. If you miss a turn, just continue uphill and keep in mind the Ski Hill Road is off to the left.

0.0 Ride up Mountain Thunder Drive and turn left onto the Morning Thunder Trail in 1/10th of a mile. This is by "The Woods at Breckenridge" sign.

0.2 Turn right on the Pence Miller Trail, just below the paved road.

0.3 Ride straight ahead and climb as the Pence Miller Trail turns off right.

0.4 Stay left and up a switchback as the Shock Hill Trail forks.

0.5 Stay left and cross a big bridge.

0.6 Continue between the condos, then turn left at a fork.

0.7 Turn left at a four-way intersection.

0.9 Ride in front of the Nordic Center and continue on singletrack.

1.0 Turn left on a straight singletrack behind a row of houses.

1.1 Turn right into the woods and follow the ditch trail.

1.3 Turn left at a fork and ride across Ski Hill Road to Peak 8 Base Area. The right fork eventually leads to the Peaks Trailhead.

1.5 Parking lot at the Peak 8 Base Area.

Option 2: To take the Four O'Clock Trail at the bottom of Sawmill Creek, turn left at mile 6.0 and ride into the woods. Turn left at the fork and over a bridge. Cross an access road and continue climbing on a singletrack marked with green signs. At the next fork, turn right and descend back to town. This trail passes the new Four O'Clock Free Ride Park. 🚲

BRECKENRIDGE SKI AREA
Loop 2: Pioneer Trail, Dwight's or the Game Trail
Ride Information ———————————————— *See map page 24*
Decription:

This ride combines the gradual 40 minute warmup climb of the Pioneer Trail with the more challenging descent of either Dwight's or the Game Trail. The high speed Game Trail winds through the woods and crosses some fun bridges. Dwight's switchbacks down ski runs and through dark conifer forests. It has some steeper, challenging drops. These two trails offer challenging but rideable ascents.

Distance: 6.5 miles descending Dwights, 7.3 miles descending The Game Trail. Both have approximately one mile of dirt road, the remainder singletrack. Add 2 miles of paved road or singletrack if you ride up from town (see Breckenridge Ski Area, Loop 1, option 1.)

——————————————————————— **Ride Information**

Time: 1-1 ½ hours

Overall Difficulty: Expert

Technical Skill: Expert

Aerobic Effort: Moderate

Elevation: Top: 11,273' Gain: 1,275'

Season: June through October

Usage: Moderate

Finding Route: Moderate, easy during the summer season with signs up. The Pioneer Trail is fairly easy to follow up as it is the most obvious path, but there are many turns and intersections. The descents are easy to follow with only a few intersections.

Location: Begin these rides at the Peak 8 Base Area, two miles up Ski Hill Road from the town of Breckenridge. To get here either drive or ride up Ski Hill Road, or try the Shock Hill Loops (see Breckenridge Ski Area, Loop 1, option 1.)

Maps: Breckenridge Ski Area summer map, available at the Peak 8 Base Area, and Latitude 40 Summit County Trails.

Mileage Log:

0.0 Begin at the base of Lifts 7 and 5 at the bottom of the Peak 8 Base. The Pioneer Trail starts to the left of Lift 5 as you look up the mountain. The trail is fairly easy to follow even though it connects several sections of road and trail, follow the most obvious path.

0.2 Stay right with the singletrack. (There is a road on the left.)

0.5 Stay right with the singletrack.

0.7 Merge left onto the dirt road.

0.8 Turn left at the fork in the road.

0.9 Ride straight ahead as a steeper spur takes off left and up.

1.0 The road narrows to a wide singletrack again.

1.3 Stay right at a fork in the trail. Follow this long straightaway north.

1.6 Ride under a lift as the singletrack again becomes doubletrack, and climb gradually. The Swinger singletrack is below you on the next ski run.

1.8 Stay left with the road around a switchback, passing the Swinger singletrack off to the right.

2.0 Turn right off the road and onto a wide trail (an old road.) This turn is just before another ski run and an intersection with a major road. Continue on a long straightaway. Pass a "Powerline Run" ski sign here.

2.2 Stay left and continue climbing, passing the Swinger Trail.

2.4 Stay right on the singletrack just before the top of a lift, and climb a couple of rocky switchbacks.

2.6 Stay left on a switchback, passing Breakaway singletrack spur off to the right.

2.8 Cross a steep road, continue on singletrack.

2.9 The trail forks, stay right.

3.4 Stay left around the switchback, passing Klinko's singletrack to the right.

3.7 Stay left with the wide singletrack, passing a road on the right.

3.8 Arrive at road intersection with Frosty's Freeway. Continue right on the Pioneer Trail and climb to the Vista House.

3.9 Just past and below the Vista House is a singletrack on the right. Begin descending.

4.3 Arrive at three-way intersection. Ride straight ahead on Dwight's Trail. (Left is the Game Trail, see option 1, below; Right is Klinko Falls.)

4.6 Stay left passing the Breakaway singletrack.

5.1 Fun bridge!

5.4 Cross a road.

5.7 Cross a road.

2.2 Turn right at the intersection with The Game Trail.

2.3 Cross the Swinger Switchbacks Trail, a road at this point.

6.5 Back to the base of the lifts.

Option 1: The Game Trail:

0.0 Begin at the base of Lifts 7 and 5 at the bottom of the Peak 8 Base. The Pioneer Trail starts to the left of Lift 5 as you look up the mountain. The trail is fairly easy to follow even though it connects several sections of road and trail, follow the most obvious path.

0.2 Stay right with the singletrack. (There is a road on the left.)

0.5 Stay right with the singletrack.

0.7 Merge left onto the dirt road.

0.8 Turn left at the fork in the road.

0.9 Ride straight ahead as a steeper spur takes off left and up.

1.0 The road narrows to a wide singletrack again.

1.3 Stay right at a fork in the trail. Follow this long straightaway north.

1.6 Ride under a lift as the singletrack again becomes doubletrack, and climb gradually. The Swinger singletrack is below you on the next ski run.

1.8 Stay left with the road around a switchback, passing the Swinger singletrack off to the right.

2.0 Turn right off the road and onto a wide trail (an old road.) This turn is just before another ski run and an intersection with a major road. Continue on a long straightaway. Pass a "Powerline Run" ski sign here.

2.2 Stay left and continue climbing, passing the Swinger Trail.

BRECKENRIDGE SKI AREA

Loop 2: Pioneer Trail, Dwight's or the Game Trail

2.4   Stay right on the singletrack just before the top of a lift, and climb a couple of rocky switchbacks.

2.6   Stay left on a switchback, passing Breakaway singletrack spur off to the right.

2.8   Cross a steep road, continue on singletrack.

2.9   The trail forks, stay right.

3.4   Stay left around the switchback, passing Klinko's singletrack to the right.

3.7   Stay left with the wide singletrack, passing a road on the right.

3.8   Arrive at road intersection with Frosty's Freeway. Continue right on the Pioneer Trail and climb to the Vista House.

3.9   Just past and below the Vista House is a singletrack on the right. Begin descending.

4.3   Arrive at a three-way intersection. Turn left onto The Game Trail and climb a short hill.

4.4   Turn right on a road that leads to the T-bar lift.

4.6   Turn right onto the singletrack at the base of the T-bar.

5.4   This section is fast and winding, switchbacking and crossing bridges, and very fun!

6.9   Ride under a quad lift and cross a road.

7.1   Dwight's Trail merges in from the right.

7.2   Cross the Swinger Switchbacks Trail, a road at this point.

7.4   Finish at the base of the lifts. 🚲

The French Gulch Trail

THE PEAKS TRAIL

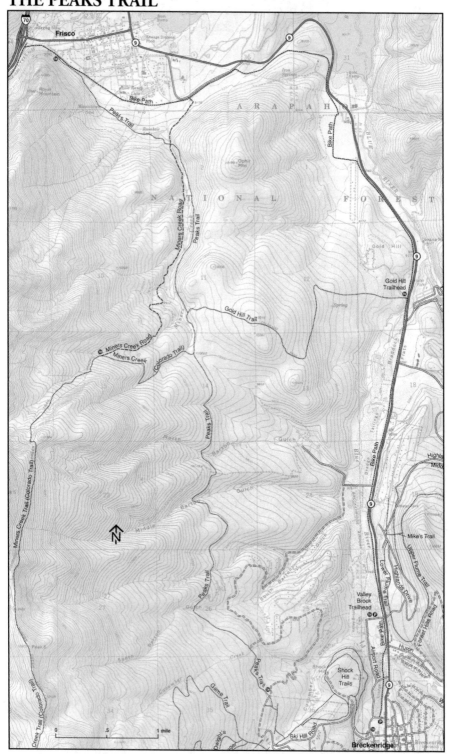

Description:

This popular ride traversing from Breckenridge to Frisco offers nice views of the Front Range fourteeners and a variety of terrain from smooth and fast to rocky and rooted, without much elevation gain. The trail is quite eroded in several places due to heavy use. I describe it as a loop, but the trail is also good as an out and back from either end, or as a shuttle ride

Distance: 18.4 mile loop, 8.4 miles of singletrack, and 10 miles of paved bike path. Add 2 miles of paved road or singletrack to get to the trailhead from Breckenridge, depending on your choice of route. See option 1, below. As an out and back, the trail is 16.8 miles of singletrack.

Time: 3-4 hours

Overall Difficulty: Advanced Intermediate

Technical Skill: Advanced Intermediate, with short expert sections

Aerobic Effort: Moderate

Elevation: Top: 10,240' Gain: 1,750'

Season: June through early October

Usage: Heavy

Finding Route: Easy, most turns are well marked. The Frisco end is a little more difficult.

Location: There are a variety of ways to get to the Peaks Trail from Breckenridge to ride it as a loop. Park in the public parking lot at the northeast corner of Ski Hill Road and South Park Road, at the Watson Trailhead. The easiest way is to ride up 2 miles on Ski Hill Road. Pass below the Peak 8 Base Area, and continue on the dirt road to the trailhead on the left. The Shock Hill Trails offer several singletrack options for riding up; see option 1 at the end of this description. To get to the trailhead in Frisco for an out and back or loop, park at the public lot for the Summit bike path system at the Junction of I70 and Main Street at the west end of Frisco. Ride the bike path for approximately ½ mile until the Farmer's Corner Trailhead. There is a picnic table and sign "Zach's Stop" here. Turn right into the parking area, the trail begins to the left.

Maps: Latitude 40 Summit County Colorado Trails or the Sky Terrain Summit, Vail and Holy Cross Map

Mileage Log:

0.0 Starting at the Peaks Trailhead off Ski Hill Road, ride onto the signed singletrack south of the parking lot. There are blue diamonds on the trees that mark the trail.

0.2 Stay on the main trail as faint spurs descend to the right.

0.6 Cross the signed Cucumber Creek and Road. Continue straight ahead on the singletrack.

1.1 Ride straight ahead on the main trail, passing a spur to the right.

THE PEAKS TRAIL
Ride Information

3.0   Arrive at the Barton ditch and ride along the bank. This is fun and fast. Continue on another ditch bank after you leave the Barton ditch.

3.9   Turn sharp left off the ditch. This turn is marked with a "Peaks" sign and arrow. Climb a short hill.

4.2   Views of Grays and Torres Peaks from the clearcut.

5.0   At the fork, turn right on the Peaks Trail. The left trail heads up Miners Creek, the route for the Colorado Trail.

5.3   Stay left and continue riding downhill, passing the Gold Hill Trail to the right. This is a fun descent along Miners Creek, mostly fast and smooth, but beware of a few technical sections and drops.

7.2   Cross Miners Creek and Road. The trail continues on the other side. Watch for other users on the remainder of the trail.

7.3   Cross an intersection of a road on one side and a trail to the lake on the other. Continue straight ahead.

7.5   Curve to the right following the edge of the lake. The trail continues just over the rise at the end of the lake.

7.6   Cross a trail, continue straight. Follow the blue diamonds.

7.8   Cross a road.

8.3   Trailhead at a junction of several trails. The paved bike path is to your right. Turn left on the singletrack to continue to Farmers Corner Trailhead parking, or turn right and ride to the bike path to return to Breckenridge.

8.4   If you continued to the Farmers Corner Trailhead, turn right to the paved path and then right on the path, heading back toward Breckenridge.

9.0   Ride straight over a private road, staying with the bike path.

9.6   Turn right at the fork in the bike path.

10.1 Stay right on the bike path.

14.0 Pass the Gold Hill Trailhead and the Colorado Trail.

17.1 Pass the Meadow Brook Road and Trailhead on the right. Continue straight toward Breckenridge.

18.4 Back to the parking lot at Watson Trailhead, and your car.

Option 1: To ride the Shock Hill Trails up from Breckenridge: Access these at the Watson Trailhead, at South Park Avenue and Ski Hill Road, across from the large public parking area. It is a bit confusing in this area because of the many trails. If you miss a turn, just continue uphill and keep in mind the Ski Hill Road is off to the left.

0.0   Ride up Mountain Thunder Drive and turn left on the Morning Thunder Trail in 1/10th of a mile. This is by "The Woods at Breckenridge" sign.

0.2   Turn right on the Pence Miller Trail, just below the paved road.

0.3   Ride straight ahead and climb as the Pence Miller Trail turns off right.

0.4 Stay left and up around a switchback as the Shock Hill Trail forks.

0.5 Stay left and cross a big bridge.

0.6 Continue between the condos, then turn left at a fork.

0.7 Turn left at a four-way intersection.

0.9 Ride in front of the Nordic Center and continue on th singletrack.

1.0 Turn left on a straight singletrack behind a row of houses.

1.1 Turn right into woods and follow the trail.

1.3 Turn right at a fork below the Peak 8 Base Area. If you end up on Ski Hill Road, ride past the base area and continue less than ½ mile on the dirt road to the signed trailhead on the left.

1.6 Pass a beaver pond on the right, then climb steeply. Merge onto a contouring trail.

1.8 Turn left and up at split.

1.9 Stay left and up a fork, then turn right on a flat flume trail.

2.0 Ride across Ski Hill Road to the Peaks Trailhead. 🚲

The Peaks Trail

THE BURRO & SPRUCE CREEK TRAILS

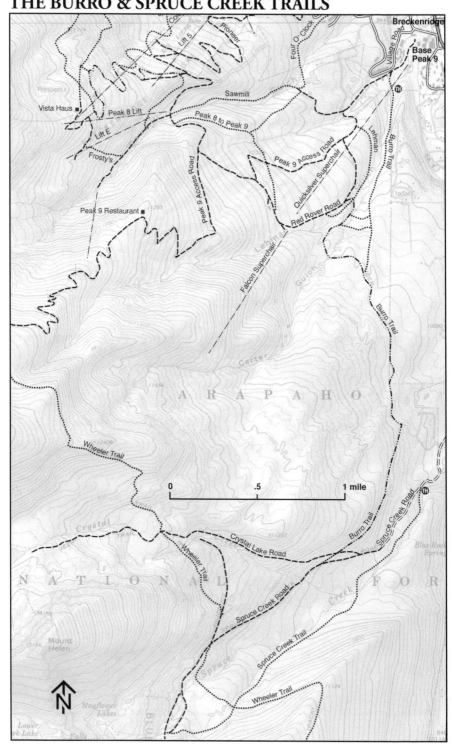

36

THE BURRO & SPRUCE CREEK TRAILS
Ride Information

Description:

This is a popular ride right out of the town of Breckenridge, combining wide old singletracks with dirt roads to make a fun, technical loop. A side trip to the beautiful Mayflower Lakes is a perfect spot for lunch and a chilly swim on a nice day. (From the top of Spruce Creek Road, turn right at either mile 4.1 or 4.6)

Distance: 10.4 mile loop, 2 miles of dirt road, 8.4 miles of singletrack and old doubletrack.

Time: 2-3 hours

Overall Difficulty: Expert

Technical Skill: Expert

Aerobic Effort: Moderately high

Elevation: Top: 11,100' Gain: 1920'

Season: Late June through October

Usage: Moderate

Finding Route: Fairly easy

Location: Begin this ride at the signed Burro Trail Trailhead, 2/10ths of a mile up the Peak 9 Service Road from the Breckenridge Peak 9 Ski Area base. Park in the public parking lots to the north and east of Ski Hill Road and South Park Road. To get to the bottom of the Peak 9 Service Road, turn left and cross Ski Hill Road, and ride south on North Park Road ¼ mile. Just past the intersection with Village Road, turn right and ride through the base area buildings, staying right and riding above Maggie's Pond. The ticket office and lift base are just above this. Ride up the service road and left across the drainage to the trailhead, about 2/10ths of a mile.

Maps: Latitude 40 Summit County Colorado Trails

Mileage Log:

0.0   Start climbing the Burro Trail. This trail is marked by blue diamonds, and follows the left bank of the creek. You will pass many spurs in the next mile, but just follow the wide, main trail. At mile 1.3 is your first major turn.

0.1   Stay right passing a steep trail to the left.

0.3   Stay left as a spur crosses the creek to the right.

0.5   Ride straight ahead as spur trails turn off to the left and right.

0.7   Pass a spur to the right and cross another trail.

1.3   Turn left at the T-intersection. This next section of old doubletrack is rocky and challenging. (Right leads to the Lehman Trail on the ski area.)

1.8   Ride straight ahead, passing a singletrack that descends to the left.

2.1   Ride straight ahead as a doubletrack descends to the left.

3.0   Cross the steep Crystal Lakes gravel road. The Burro Trail narrows to a singletrack.

Ride Information

3.1   Intersect Spruce Creek Road. Turn right and ride up the steady climb of this gravelly road.

4.0   The Wheeler Trail crosses Spruce Creek Road. Continue straight up on the Spruce Creek Road. (Left on the Wheeler Trail also leads to the Spruce Creek Trail. Right on the Wheeler Trail is a very difficult climb with quite a bit of hike-a-bike.)

4.1   Stay left with the main road when a fork turns off to the right.

4.3   After a short descent, the road climbs quite steeply.

4.6   Turn left onto the signed Spruce Creek Trail, across from a pullout and small concrete structure.

5.1   Ride straight across the signed Wheeler Trail

6.2   Cross Spruce Creek.

6.5   Cross a road, continue straight ahead. Look for the slash on the trees that mark the trail.

6.7   Stay left and ride up over a rocky area, passing a spur to the right. (The right fork looks more obvious, but don't get fooled.)

6.8   Reach the Spruce Creek Trailhead. Turn left and up Spruce Creek Road. Stay right or left at the road fork ahead, the unsigned Burro Trail crosses both.

7.3   (Approx mileage) Turn right onto the Burro Trail and retrace your tread back to the ski area.

10.4   Back at the Burro Trailhead. 🚲

The Wheeler Trail

The Colorado Trail, between Horseshoe Gulch and Highway 9

WHEELER & MINERS CREEK TRAILS

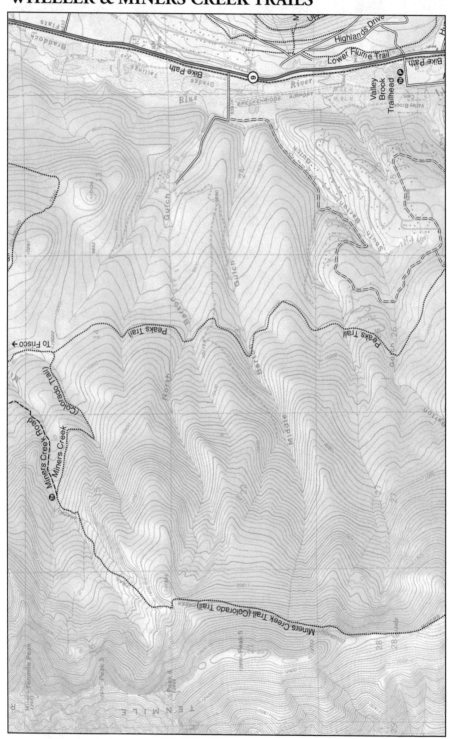

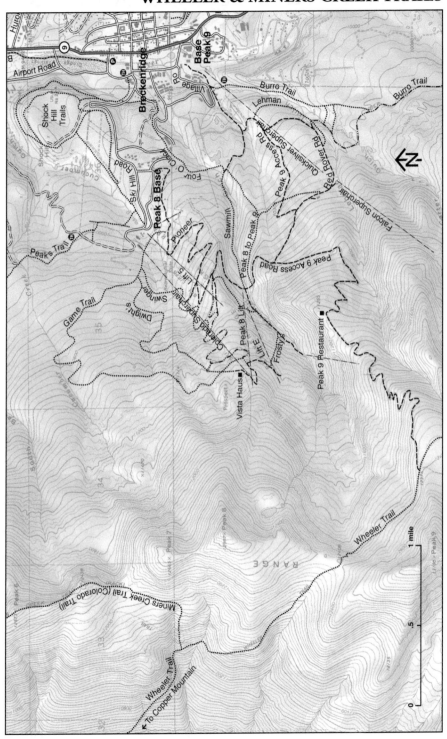

WHEELER & MINERS CREEK TRAILS
Ride Information

Description:

The Wheeler and Miners Creek Trails offer amazing views from atop the Ten Mile Range and challenging riding in a wilderness-like setting. Expect to see raptors and small wildlife along the way, but hardly any other riders once past the ski area. The ride starts with a long climb up the Breckenridge Ski Area toward Peaks 8 and 9. The Wheeler Trail rolls through a mountain cirque, up and over a high pass, and descends steeply to a smooth, contouring section high above The Snake River Valley. From here the loop takes the Miners Creek Trail up to a high altitude traverse of the Ten Mile Range. Expect to walk some, as the trail passes through talus fields and tundra at 12,000 feet and above. The descent into Miners Creek is beautiful and the trail is rocky and rooted. Finish this loop with either the Peaks Trail or The Gold Hill Trail, see option 3. To shorten the ride, continue descending the Wheeler Trail to Copper Mountain, see option 2. The Wheeler Trail is a fun adventure in the opposite direction as well, see option 1.

Distance: 22 mile loop, 5.7 miles of dirt road and 16.3 miles of singletrack.

Time: 4 ½ -7 hours

Overall Difficulty: Epic, Expert for option 2.

Technical Skill: Expert

Aerobic Effort: Strenuous

Elevation: Top: 12,570'Gain: 4,890', Option 2: Top 12,460' Gain: 3,490'

Season: July through September

Usage: Light

Finding Route: Easy-Moderate

Location: To start this ride, park in the public lots at the northeast corner of Ski Hill Road and South Park Avenue, near the Watson Trailhead. Turn left on South Park Avenue and cross Ski Hill Road. Continue on North Park Avenue for 3/10th of a mile and turn right into "The Village." You will know you are in the right spot when you soon see Ticket Sales, Ski School, and Maggie Pond. Start at the Base of the Peak 9 Superchair and ticket sales, just to the right and uphill of the main plaza. Village Road will also take you to the access road, turn right off Park Road and continue up ¼ mile, turn left before Beaver Run Resort and ride to the access road.

Maps: Latitude 40 Summit County Colorado Trails

Mileage Log:

0.0 Start riding on the dirt access road that leads under the 6-person chair lift. The climb up this road is moderate and steady until reaching The Peak 9 Restaurant.

0.3 Pass the Beaver Run Resort and Superchair on the right. Continue climbing on road.

0.6 Pass Peak 8 Superconnect on the right.

0.7 Pass the Lehman Trail on the left.

0.9   The road splits, turn left on Red Rover Road.

1.3   Pass Ten Mile Station on the right and the Falcon Superchair and a spur road on the left.

1.5   Pass a singletrack to the right.

1.6   Pass the Peak 8 to Peak 9 Singletrack on the right.

1.7   Stay right at the road fork and ride above a concrete block building, then under a lift.

1.8   Turn left and up when road splits.

2.2   Stay left and continue climbing up around a switchback when a spur heads to the right and steeply down.

3.4   Stay right and continue climbing at the fork.

3.5   Turn right and up toward the Peak 9 Restaurant.

3.6   Ride to the left of the restaurant and stay with the main road, riding toward Wheeler Pass. The road begins to climb more steeply and becomes quite rocky.

4.1   Ride straight ahead above the Mercury Superchair, passing a spur to the right.

5.7   Turn right on the Wheeler Trail. This turn is before the summit of the ridge. From here traverse the tundra below Peak 9 and climb to the saddle. See option 1 for a left turn onto The Wheeler Trail.

6.7   Summit of Wheeler Pass, with Peak 8 to the right and Peak 9 to the left. 12,460 feet! Nice view of Copper Mountain Ski Area and the Gore Mountains. Descend steeply for 4/10ths of a mile and then roll along the smooth, mostly level trail through the forest.

8.1   Turn right on the Miners Creek Trail (The Colorado Trail.) (Left descends to Copper Mountain, see option 2.) This is a difficult climb. After reaching a saddle, enjoy a beautiful traverse along the steep meadow hillsides.

10.0   Reach the saddle on the main ridge and head left over the talus. Pick up the faint trail that continues north along the top of the ridge.

10.6   Descend some challenging switchbacks and traverse high above the Blue River Valley.

12.0   Come to a lower saddle above Miners Creek, Peak 4 and 3 to the left. Descend this technical and challenging trail.

13.9   Arrive at the junction with the Miners Creek Road. Stay right and continue on the trail.

15.3   Junction with the Peaks Trail. Turn right and ride south toward Breckenridge. (Or see option 3 to finish the loop on the Gold Hill Trail.)

16.1   Descend through a clearcut. Views of Grays and Torres Peaks to the left.

16.4   Sharp right onto a ditch bank trail section.

19.2   Stay right on the main trail. Spurs drop off the bank to the left.

WHEELER & MINERS CREEK TRAILS
Ride Information

19.7 Cross a road and Cucumber Creek.

20.1 Stay on the main trail, more spurs descending to the left.

20.3 Reach the Peaks Trailhead. Turn right and ride 2 miles down Ski Hill Road, or try the Shock Hill singletracks, directly across from the Peaks Trail. Take this and descend to the right toward Breckenridge. Keep in mind ski hill road is to the right while you explore the many spurs on the descent.

Option 1: Wheeler Trail to the Burro Trail or McCullough Gulch

Follow the directions above to mile 5.7 and turn left on the Wheeler Trail. Use navigational skill to cross the tundra, as the trail is faint at first. This first section is very rocky and expect to carry your bike. Descend to Spruce Creek Road. To take the Burro Trail back to Breckenridge, turn left and downhill, then left on the unsigned singletrack in 9/10th of a mile. (See Burro Trail, page 37) To continue on the Wheeler Trail, ride straight across Spruce Creek Road. Cross the Spruce Creek Trail shortly, and enjoy a much more moderate section of the trail. When you reach McCullough Gulch Road, return as you came back to the Spruce Creek Trail, then from here ride back to Breckenridge by the Spruce Creek Trail and the Burro Trail. I don't recommend riding Highway 9 back, because this busy road is narrow without much shoulder.

Option 2: The Wheeler Trail to Copper Mountain

Follow the above directions to mile 8.1, stay left and descend steeply to Ten Mile Creek. Turn right at the trail intersection at approximately mile 9.7, just before a bridge. Follow the old doubletrack along the creek 1 mile and cross a big concrete bridge. Turn right on the paved recreation path and follow it back approximately 5 ½ miles to the Peaks Trailhead behind Frisco. Either ride the paved path back to Breckenridge, or take the Peaks Trail back. (See Peaks Trail, page 33.) This loop is about 25 miles long and takes 4-5 hours.

Option 3: To take the Gold Hill Trail and the bike path back to Breckenridge from the intersection of Miners Creek Trail and The Peaks Trail: Ride to mile 15.3 in the above description.

15.3 Turn left on the Peaks Trail.

15.6 Turn right, staying with the Miners Creek Trail. Look for the Colorado trail markers. This is a very rocky trail, and a challenging climb.

16.6 Top out and begin a fast descent. Follow blue diamond markers on the trees.

16.8 Cross an old doubletrack.

17.2 Cut left into a clearcut.

17.9 Continue on a singletrack, crossing an old road.

18.9 Turn right on County Road 950 and arrive at the Gold Hill Trailhead. Turn right and return to Breckenridge on the paved recreation path.

23.2 Back to the parking lot. ᚖ

The Miners Creek Trail

The Wheeler Trail, approaching Wheeler Saddle

THE COLORADO TRAIL-HORSESHOE GULCH

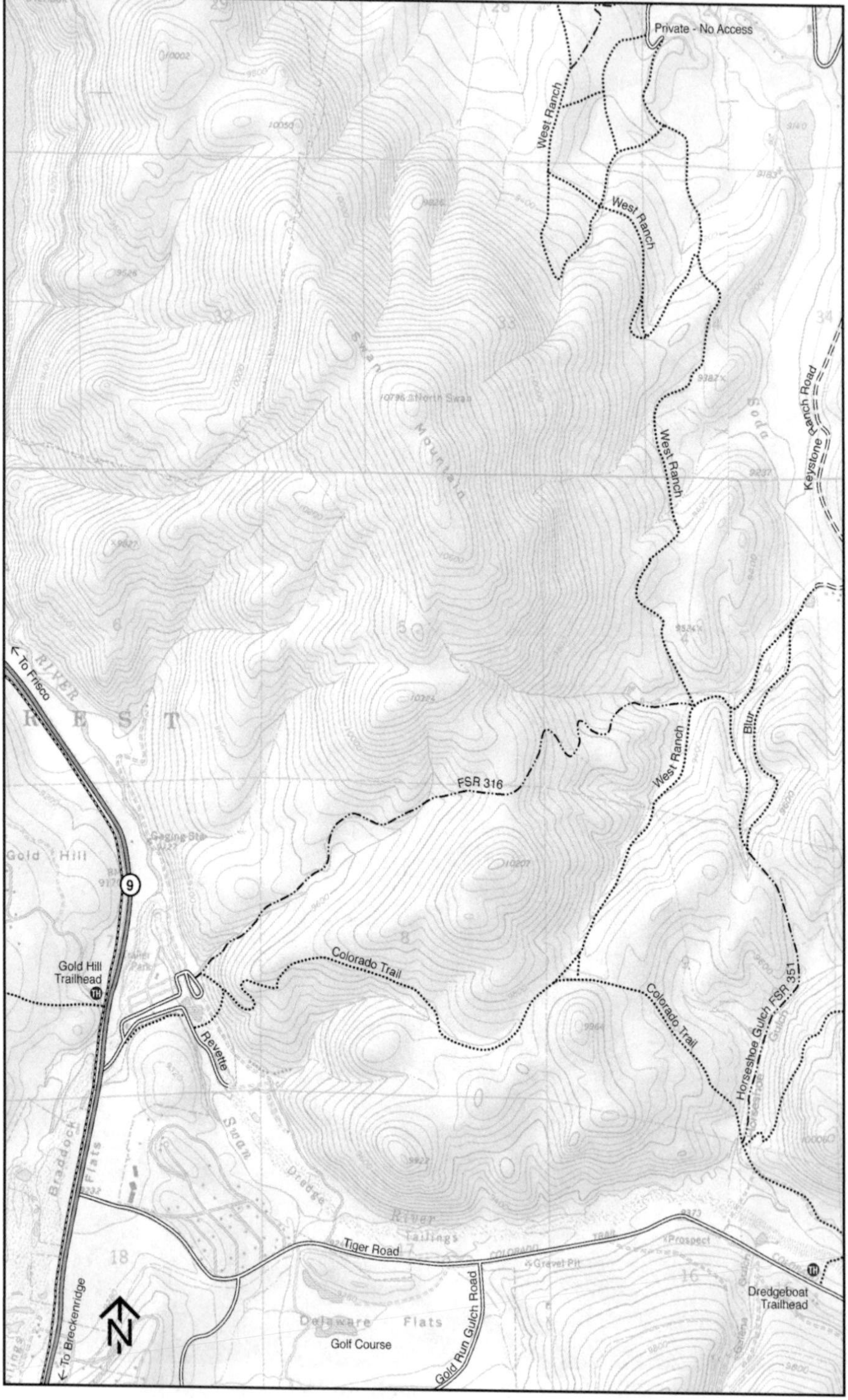

West Loop

West Loop

West Ridge (Colorado Trail)

Colorado Trail

Keystone Gulch Road

Keystone Gulch Road

Red's Trail

Ranch Trail

Tiger Road

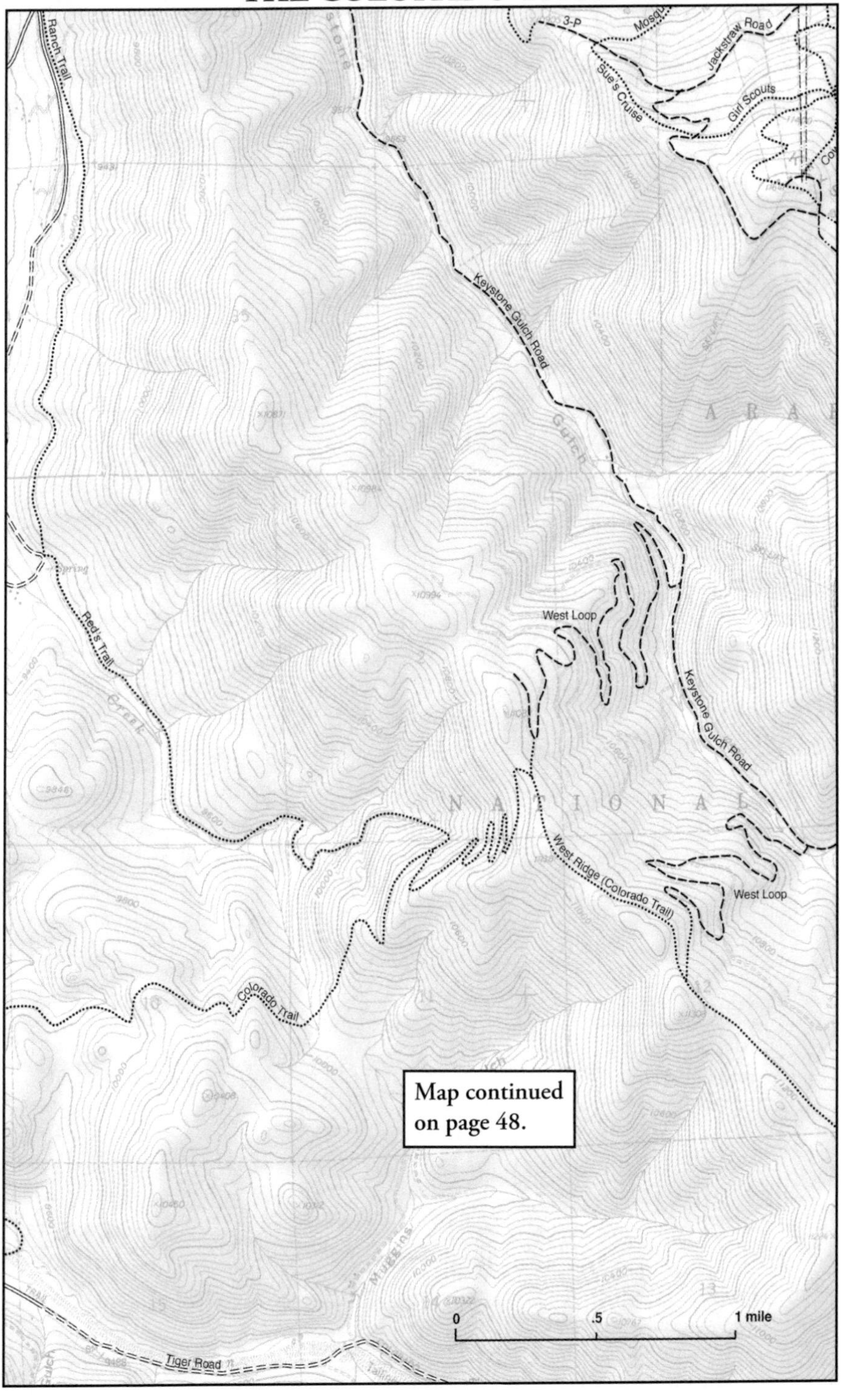

Map continued on page 48.

0   .5   1 mile

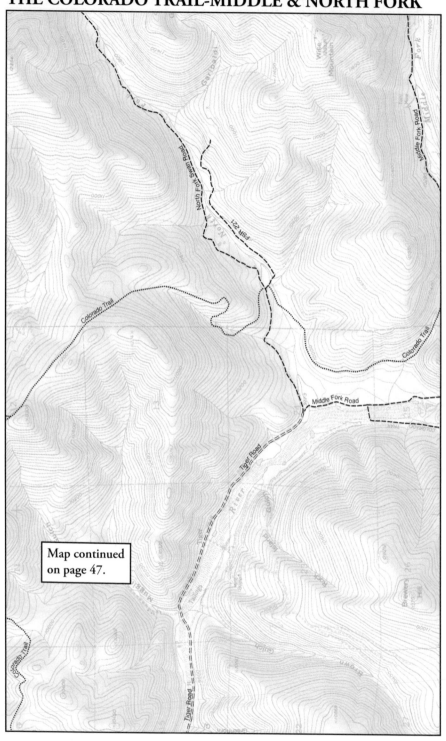

Map continued on page 47.

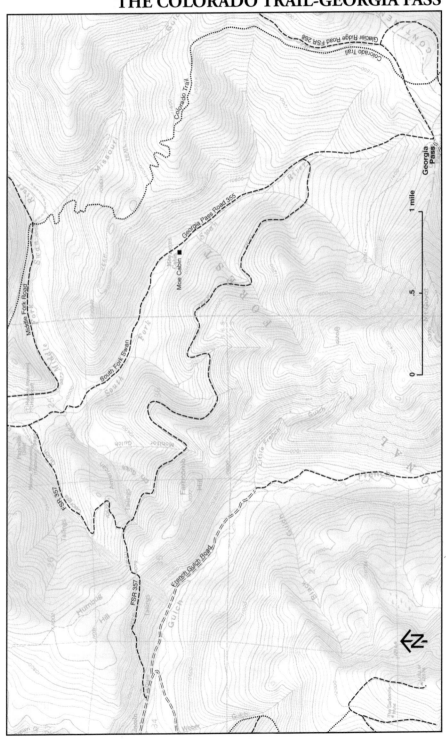

HORSESHOE GULCH TO THE COLORADO TRAIL
Ride Information ————————————— *See map page 46*

Description:

This fast, smooth, non-motorized singletrack ride starts just north of Breckenridge on Tiger Road. The descent will make you smile with its banked corners and hardpacked surface. The ride starts with a road warm-up, and is followed by a wonderful, mostly intermediate trail through meadows and woods. One steep descent and climb, and a few steep switchbacks at the end will challenge your skills, but are also easily walked. This loop is challenging and fun in reverse, but watch for downhillers. There are many other ways to link up trails here to make a loop, have fun exploring! See The Rossater and West Ranch Trails, page 85, and The Colorado Trail: Keystone Gulch to West Ridge, page 80, for more information.

Distance: 9.4 mile loop, 3.4 miles of paved road and bike path, 6 miles of sweet singletrack!

Time: 1 ½-2 hours

Overall Difficulty: Intermediate to Advanced Intermediate

Technical Skill: Intermediate to Advanced Intermediate

Aerobic Effort: Moderate

Elevation: Top: 9,800' Gain: 900'

Season: Late May through October

Usage: Moderate. Be courteous to other users on these popular trails.

Finding Route: Moderate

Location: Start this ride at the Gold Hill Trailhead. to get here, drive 3 ½ miles north of Breckenridge's French Street on Highway 9, and turn left on County Road 950. The trailhead is just off the highway. From Frisco, drive south about 4 ½ miles or 7 miles from the junction of Highway 9 and I70 to County Road 950 and the trailhead.

Maps: Sky Terrain Summit, Vail and Holy Cross. Latitude 40 Summit County is missing one of the trails on this ride, but is still useful.

Mileage Log:

0.0 Ride south toward Breckenridge on the paved recreation path.

0.2 Ride straight ahead on the bike path, passing Revette Drive and The Colorado Trail to the left.

0.6 Turn left and cross Highway 9. Begin riding east on Tiger Road.

3.2 Turn left into the somewhat obscure Dredgeboat Trailhead parking lot on the left. This is just past a huge old dredgeboat, also on the left, and just before the end of the pavement. Ride over the old dredge piles on the trail.

3.4 Cross the creek and turn left. Follow the creek down briefly, then turn right and climb on an old doubletrack.

3.6 Ride around the closed gate.

3.7 Cross the Colorado Trail, and climb gradually on the doubletrack into beautiful open meadows. The trail narrows to singletrack. (To shorten the ride and make it easier, just turn left on the Colorado Trail and follow it back to the Gold Hill Trailhead.)

4.7 The trail forks, turn left and descend a steep hill. (Right leads to Keystone Ranch Road, via the Blur Trail.)

5.2 Turn left at the T-intersection and ride up the creek. (Right leads to Keystone Ranch Road.)

5.4 Stay left at another intersection, heading toward the powerlines. Climb a long, challenging singletrack hill. (Right leads toward Summit Cove on the West Ranch Trail.)

6.4 Turn right on the Colorado Trail.

6.6 Ride through an open gate and start an awesome downhill. This was made for mountain biking, it is so fast and fun!

8.0 Start some sharp switchbacks.

8.5 Turn left sharply as a spur trail forks off to the right of a switchback. Descend to a motorhome park. (The right spur leads to Forest Service 316.)

8.7 Stay right at the condos, ride around the pond, and cross a bridge.

8.8 Turn right on Revette Road and follow it briefly, then turn left onto the Colorado Trail. The singletrack parallels the road.

9.2 Merge left onto the road and ride straight across Highway 9. Turn right on the paved bike path.

9.4 Back to the Gold Hill Trailhead. 🚲

THE COLORADO TRAIL
Middle & North Fork

See map page 46-49 ———————————— **Ride Information**

Description:

If you only have one ride to do in Summit County, pick a section of the Colorado Trail. It is all great riding, and this is no exception. This loop is of moderate length and difficulty, and has a whole lot of smooth, winding descent for your riding pleasure! The Colorado Trail is obvious and easy to follow. Look for the small double peaked symbols on the trees. This loop starts with a warm-up on the Tiger and Middle Fork of the Swan Roads, and then climbs and descends gradually on singletrack to the North Fork of the Swan. From here to the West Ridge the trail climbs continuously for two miles. Beyond the West Ridge the trail is all fast, rolling, fun, and almost entirely downhill. For a longer version of this ride, see The Colorado Trail: Georgia Pass, page 54, and for a shorter version starting up the North Fork drainage, see option page 53. The trail is also accessible from Horseshoe Gulch at the Dredgeboat Trailhead, see page 50. The Colorado Trail in the opposite direction from The Gold Hill Trailhead (see location, below) is also good riding. There is dispersed camping up The North and Middle Fork Roads, and up Georgia Pass as well.

Distance: Middle Fork: 25 mile loop, 16 miles of singletrack, 3.5 miles of pavement, 5.5 miles of dirt road. North Fork: 21 mile loop, 14.5 miles of singletrack, 3.5 miles of pavement, 3 miles of dirt road.

Time: 3-4 hours

Overall Difficulty: Advanced Intermediate to expert due to the climb to West Ridge.

Technical Skill: Advanced Intermediate

Aerobic Effort: Moderately high

Elevation: Middle Fork: Top: 11,260' Gain: 3,080'

North Fork: Top:11,260' Gain: 2,780'

Season: June through early October

Usage: Moderate

Finding Route: Easy

Location: Start at The Gold Hill Trailhead. This is located 3.6 miles north of French Street (at the north end of Breckenridge) on the left side of Highway 9 on County Road 950. The trailhead is 4.5 miles south of Frisco and 7 miles south of the junction of Highway 9 and I70. If you ride from town on the bike path, turn right onto Tiger Road 3 miles north of Breckenridge, at mile 0.6, below.

Maps: Latitude 40 Summit County Colorado Trails or the Sky Terrain Summit, Vail, and Holy Cross Map.

Mileage Log:

0.0   From The Gold Hill Trailhead, ride south toward Breckenridge on the paved Blue River Recreation Path.

0.2   Ride straight ahead on the bike path, passing Revette Road and The Colorado Trail on the left.

0.6   Turn left and cross Highway 9 to Tiger Road. You will be on this road for a few miles.

3.2   Pass the Dredgeboat Trailhead on the left. This leads to Horseshoe Gulch, also access to the Colorado Trail.

3.4   End of the pavement, continue straight.

5.6   Pass a heavily used campsite on the right.

6.6   Stay right and cross a bridge, passing the North Fork of the Swan Road to the left. This also accesses the Colorado Trail, see option 1.

7.0   Ride straight ahead at the fork, staying on the Middle Fork of Swan River Road 6. This road climbs very gradually.

7.8 The road forks, stay left on the Middle Fork Road.

8.9 Turn left on the signed Colorado Trail. This turn is just after the section of the Colorado Trail from Georgia Pass comes in on the right. There is a campsite on the right. The upper section to Georgia Pass is a challenging climb and fast descent if ridden as an out and back from here.

11.3 Cross a creek and stay right along the creek through the campsites and braided trails.

11.5 Turn left away from the creek in the last campsite and onto an old ditch bank. Cross the North Fork Road and continue on the ditch bank.

11.6 The trail turns right, off the ditch.

11.9 Cross a small creek, stay above a campsite, and ride around the top of an old pole fence. Begin to switchback up gradually.

14.1 The trail levels, then descends. Views of The Keystone Ski Area are to the right.

14.6 Turn left at the fork, staying with the Colorado Trail. The right fork descends to Keystone Gulch Road.

15.7 Stay left at another fork and begin long switchbacks down. Right also descends to Keystone Gulch Road.

18.1 Turn sharp left in a sage meadow. Descend to cross a creek, climb shortly, and then zoom downhill! (Straight ahead leads to Soda Ridge Road on The Red's, West Ranch, and Aqueduct Trails, also an excellent ride. See Keystone Gulch to West Ridge Loop, page 80.)

19.6 Turn right at the trail fork.

20.8 Ride straight across an old doubletrack in Horseshoe Gulch, then right and uphill.

22.2 Stay left when a trail comes in from below.

22.3 Top out and begin a fast, winding awesome section of downhill!

24.2 Turn sharp left above a motorhome village.

24.3 Stay right at the condos, ride around the pond, and cross a bridge.

24.4 Turn right on the paved road, then left onto the The Colorado Trail.

24.7 Descend to the road and turn left.

24.8 Ride across Highway 9, and turn right onto the bike path.

25.1 Back to The Gold Hill Trailhead.

Option: To ride this trail from the North Fork of the Swan Road, follow the above directions to mile 6.6. This ride is not easier, but is 4 miles shorter.

6.6 Turn left before the bridge and ride up the North Fork of the Swan Road.

7.1 Pass a campsite on the left, then round a corner and pass more camping on the right. Pass Forest Road 221. Ride through a gate and stay left.

7.4 Turn left onto the marked Colorado Trail. From here you are at mile 11.5 of the previous directions for the Middle Fork. Subtract 4.1 miles from each mile point on the Middle Fork description for your mileage. 🚲

THE COLORADO TRAIL
Georgia Pass Loop

Ride Information ——————————— *See map page 46-49*

Description:

This is a wonderful section of the Colorado Trail (CT) to do on a bright summer day! There is so much fun descending, rolled out perfectly for cross-country mountain biking, that you are guaranteed to be giggling at the end! This outstanding ride begins with a long road ride, at first flat and easy, then becoming very steep and challenging once you cross the South Fork of the Swan at mile 8. After 12 miles, riders are rewarded with great views of The South Park, and 20 miles of awesome singletrack. The section from Glacier Ridge (just above Georgia Pass) to the Middle Fork of the Swan River Road is smooth and contouring along the high ridge, then a very fast descent. A technical section brings you to the Middle Fork Road. The next section is short, rolling and fast, followed by a sustained two mile climb from The North Fork to the West Ridge. From here riders spin along the top and roll down an awesome, long descent into the Soda Creek drainage. The trail then climbs and descends smoothly in and out of drainages and ends with some steep switchbacks down to the Gold Hill Trailhead. As an option to avoid the motor vehicle congestion on the upper Georgia Pass Road, follow directions to the Colorado Trail, Middle Fork, page 51, and ride up to Glacier Ridge and back on the upper section of The Colorado Trail, then continue back to Breckenridge on the middle and lower sections of the CT. Riding this entire CT section from The Gold Hill Trailhead as an out and back is a beautiful and challenging all singletrack ride. For shorter versions of the Georgia Pass loop, see Colorado Trail Middle Fork, page 51, and Keystone Gulch to West Ridge, page 80.

Distance: 33 mile loop, 4 miles of paved road and bike path, 9 miles of dirt road, and 20 miles of sweet singletrack!

Time: 5-7 hours

Overall Difficulty: Expert

Technical Skill: Expert

Aerobic Effort: Strenuous

Elevation: Top: 11,800' Gain: 4,700'

Season: Late June through early October

Usage: Heavy road usage on weekends, moderate trail usage. The CT is non-motorized.

Finding Route: Easy to moderate. The CT is well marked and easy to follow. Look for the small double peaked symbols on trees. The road has many unmarked spurs once you cross the South Fork of the Swan River, follow the directions closely.

Location: Start at the Gold Hill Trailhead. This is located 3.6 miles north of French Street (at the north end of Breckenridge) on the left or west side of Highway 9 on County Road 950. The trailhead is 4.5 miles south of Frisco or 7 miles south of the junction of Highway 9 and I70, on the right.

Maps: Latitude 40 Summit County Colorado Trails, and The Sky Terrain Trail Map Summit, Vail and Holy Cross. I suggest taking both.

THE COLORADO TRAIL
Georgia Pass Loop

Mileage Log:

0.0   Ride south toward Breckenridge on the paved recreation path.

0.2   Ride straight ahead on the bike path, passing Revette Road and The Colorado Trail on the left.

0.6   Turn left and cross Highway 9 to Tiger Road. You will be on this road for a few miles.

3.2   Pass the Dredgeboat Trailhead on the left.

3.4   End pavement, continue straight.

5.6   Pass a heavily used campsite on the right.

6.6   Stay right and cross a bridge, passing the North Fork of the Swan Road to the left. (This also accesses the Colorado Trail. See Colorado Trail, Middle Fork, option, page 53.)

7.0   The road forks. Turn right toward Georgia Pass and the South Fork of the Swan on Forest Road 355. Cross the dredged area and the river. (The Middle Fork Road to the left also accesses The Colorado Trail, see Colorado Trail, Middle Fork page 51. This accesses the CT to ride as an out and back on the upper section to Georgia Pass.)

7.1   Turn left after the river and start climbing.

7.7   Stay left on the main road, passing a spur to the right.

8.0   At the intersection, turn left and cross the bridge over the South Fork of the Swan River, staying on Forest Road 355. The right fork is Forest Road 357.

9.9   Ride straight ahead on 355 at the fork, passing a spur to the right. The road becomes steeper and quite rocky.

10.1   Ride straight ahead at a fork in the road, passing a spur to the left, and cross a creek. Climb steeply.

10.2   Stay right at the road fork.

10.4   Stay left on the main road.

10.8   The road forks again. Turn left and stay with Forest Road 355 toward Georgia Pass. Ride down briefly through a small meadow, and again climb steeply until Georgia Pass.

11.7   Ride straight ahead toward the pass. Pass 355A on the left, and a dead end road on the right.

11.8   Georgia Pass on the Continental Divide: 11, 585 feet. Nice views of the South Park straight ahead. Turn left and climb on the signed Forest Road 268 toward the Colorado Trail and Glacier Ridge.

12.3   Turn left onto the signed Colorado Trail. Roll smoothly along the ridge, then drop into the dark woods.

15.3   Cross a doubletrack. Stay with the trail.

15.7   Cross an unmarked singletrack.

THE COLORADO TRAIL
Georgia Pass Loop

Ride Information

17.1 Cross a log bridge and stay left, then cross another bridge.

17.2 Intersect the Middle Fork Road. Turn right and then immediately left onto the Colorado Trail.

19.6 Cross The North Fork, and stay right along the creek through the campsites.

19.8 Turn left away from the creek at the last campsite and ride onto an old ditch bank. Cross the North Fork Road, and continue on the trail.

19.9 The trail turns right off the ditch.

20.2 Cross a small creek, ride above a campsite, and around an old pole fence. Begin to switchback up gradually.

22.4 The trail levels, then descends. View of Keystone Ski Area are on the right.

22.9 Turn left at the fork, staying with the Colorado Trail. The right fork descends to Keystone Gulch Road on old doubletrack.

24.0 Turn left at another fork and begin long switchbacks down. Right also descends to Keystone Gulch Road on old doubletrack.

26.4 Turn sharp left in the sage meadow. Descend and cross a creek, climb a short hill, and then descend more! (Right leads to Soda Ridge Road and Keystone on the Red's and Aqueduct Trails. This is also a great ride, see Keystone Gulch to West Ridge page 80.)

27.9 Stay right at an unmarked trail fork.

29.1 Ride straight across an old doubletrack in Horseshoe Gulch, turn right and ride uphill on singletrack.

30.3 Stay left when a trail comes in from below.

30.4 Top out and ride through a gate. Begin a fast, winding, awesome descent!

32.3 Turn sharp left above the motorhome village.

32.4 Stay right at condos, ride around the pond, and cross a bridge. Turn right on the paved road.

32.5 Turn left on The Colorado Trail.

32.9 Merge onto the road.

33.0 Ride straight across Highway 9, and turn right onto the bike path.

33.3 Back to the Gold Hill Trailhead. 🚲

The Colorado Trail: Georgia Pass

The Colorado Trail: Middle Fork Section

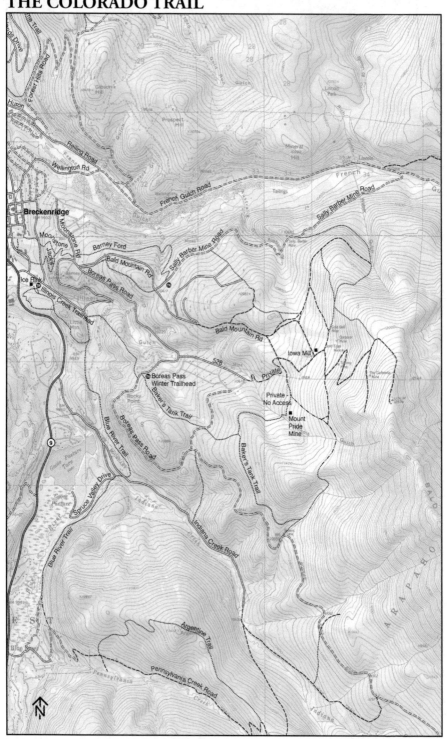

FRENCH GULCH TRAIL • MOUNT GUYOT LOOP
THE COLORADO TRAIL

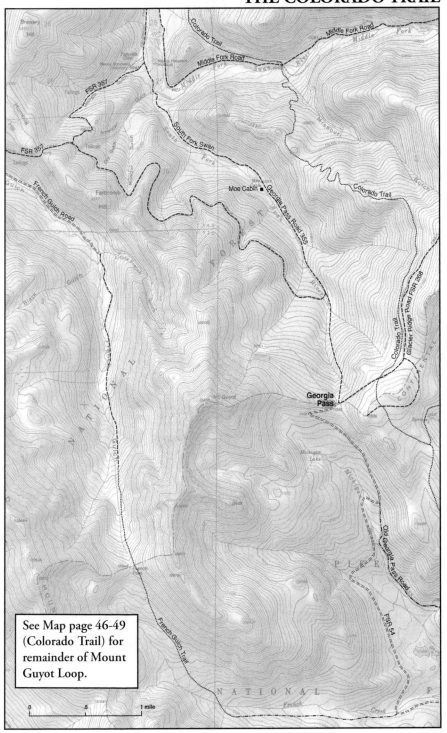

See Map page 46-49 (Colorado Trail) for remainder of Mount Guyot Loop.

FRENCH GULCH & the MOUNT GUYOT LOOP THE COLORADO TRAIL
Ride Information

Description:

This beautiful out and back in French Gulch or loop connecting to the Colorado Trail on Georgia Pass starts with a long, gradual dirt road through French Gulch. After mile 4.7, it becomes a non-motorized recreational doubletrack, and starts to climb, becoming more steep and challenging as it progresses. Near the top the ride is very challenging and it is difficult to clear the last couple hills. The views from the summit of French Pass are incredible! From here, either return the way you came, or for an epic day continue down the singletrack into the South Park and connect to the Colorado Trail by way of a smooth dirt road up to Georgia Pass. The section from French Pass down into the South Park has a wilderness feel to it, well worth the effort of climbing back up to Georgia Pass. The trail rolls past large stands of Bristlecone Pine. After reaching Georgia Pass, riders can bail in several places in the event of bad weather, fatigue, or mechanicals. The descent on the Colorado Trail is 22 miles of smooth, awesome singletrack, with only one significant climb to the West Ridge. The Colorado Trail is also non-motorized. The loop is a nice ride in the opposite direction, a little more strenuous if you climb the entire Colorado Trail singletrack.

Distance: 16.8 miles as an out and back; 2 miles of pavement, 9.8 miles of dirt road, 5 miles of primitive doubletrack. 40 miles as a loop with the Colorado Trail; 4 miles of pavement, 10 miles of dirt road, 4 miles of primitive doubletrack and 22 miles of awesome singletrack!

Time: 2½-3½ hours as an out and back, 6-8 hours as a loop with The Colorado Trail.

Overall Difficulty: As an out and back: expert. As a loop with the Colorado Trail: epic

Technical Skill: Expert

Aerobic Effort: Strenuous

Elevation: Out and Back: Top: 12,046' Gain: 2,500' Loop: Top: 12,046' Gain: 6,150'

Season: July through September

Usage: Low to moderate

Finding Route: Easy

Location: Start in the town of Breckenridge. There is a large parking lot to the northeast of Ski Hill Road and South Park Road. From here, either ride east through the parking lot toward Main Street and turn left, or turn left on Ski Hill Road and left on Main Street, to Wellington Road. Wellington Road is next to the Racers Edge Bike Shop.

Maps: Latitude 40 Summit County Colorado Trails, or Sky Terrain Summit, Vail and Holy Cross

Mileage Log:

0.0   Begin riding east up Wellington Road.

1.0   Turn right on French Gulch Road at the end of Wellington Road. Climb on this road for about 1 ½-2 hours.

1.2   Pass access to the Golden Horseshoe area on the left.

4.7   Ride around a gate.

6.0   The road gradually becomes more primitive and rugged. Ride through creek-side meadows.

6.7   Start climbing steeply into the forest. The road splits, take either fork.

6.9   The roads rejoin at a permanent road closure and locked gate. The road gradually narrows, and the climbing becomes more intense and sustained past this gate. Enjoy the beautiful high altitude meadows.

8.4   Summit of French Pass! Nice views into the French Creek drainage and The South Park. Mount Guyot is to the left, Boreas Mountain is to the right. From here return the way you came, or for a more epic ride descend straight ahead into the South Park on awesome singletrack, as described here.

9.9   Arrive at an old yellow gate. Continue right and cross two small creeks, then climb to an old logging road.

10.0   Turn left on the old logging road.

10.4   Stay left and continue downhill, passing a spur road to the right.

11.9   End of the trail on County Road 54. Turn left and begin climbing to Georgia Pass.

15.5   Ride straight ahead, passing spur road 54J on the left.

15.6   Continue climbing, passing spur road 54I on the left.

15.9   Arrive at Georgia Pass. (Left here on FS Road 355 is a bailout option, but the Colorado Trail is much more fun and isn't any more climbing than the road. The Middle Fork at mile 21.2 is a better bailout.) Continue straight ahead and onto Forest Road 268, climbing toward the signed Glacier Ridge and Colorado Trail.

16.3   Turn left onto the signed Colorado Trail singletrack. This is a smooth, contouring section, followed by a steeper, fast descent into the Middle Fork of the Swan River drainage. The trail is well marked with double-peaked Colorado Trail symbols on the trees, and easy to follow.

19.3   Cross a doubletrack. Stay with the trail. (This doubletrack is a heinous rocky four- wheeler track that leads to Georgia Pass Road.)

19.7   Cross an unmarked singletrack.

21.1   Cross a log bridge and stay left, then cross another bridge.

21.2   Turn right on the Middle Fork of the Swan River Road, and immediately left on The Colorado Trail. This section climbs and descends gradually on

FRENCH GULCH & the MOUNT GUYOT LOOP
THE COLORADO TRAIL
Ride Information

smooth singletrack! (The Middle Fork Road is a good bailout. It is an easy, flat road out.)

23.6 Stay right along the creek through the campsites and braided trails.

23.8 Turn left away from the creek in the last campsite and onto an old ditch bank. Cross the North Fork of the Swan River Road and continue on the Colorado Trail. (The North Fork Road is a very quick exit. The next section has a fairly strenuous two-mile climb up to the West Ridge.)

23.9 The trail turns right, off the ditch.

24.2 Cross a small creek above a campsite, and ride around the top of an old pole fence. Switchback gradually up. Continue climbing for 2.2 miles.

26.4 The trail levels, and descends. Views of Keystone Ski Area are on the right.

26.9 Turn left at the fork, staying with the Colorado Trail. The right fork descends by old doubletrack to Keystone Gulch Road.

28.0 Stay left at another fork and begin long switchbacks down. Right descends to Keystone Gulch Road by old doubletrack.

30.4 Turn sharp left in a sage meadow. Descend to cross a creek, climb a short hill and then enjoy more fast downhill. (Straight at this fork leads to Keystone Ranch Road via the Red's Trail, also a great ride. See Colorado Trail, Keystone Gulch to West Ridge, page 80.)

31.9 Turn right at the fork in the trail.

33.1 Ride across an old doubletrack, turn right and climb. (This doubletrack is the Horseshoe Gulch Trail and left leads to Tiger Road.)

34.3 Stay left when a trail comes in from below.

34.4 Top out and begin a fast section of downhill.

36.3 Turn sharp left above the motorhome village.

36.4 Stay right at the condos, ride around the pond, and cross a bridge. Turn right on the paved road.

36.5 Turn left on The Colorado Trail.

36.9 Ride straight onto Revette Road.

37.0 Ride straight across Highway 9 and turn left onto the paved bike path toward Breckenridge. The bike path will take you directly to the parking lots.

40.0 Back to your car. ᛇ

French Gulch

French Gulch Trail (Mt. Guyot Loop)

COLORADO TRAIL: KENOSHA PASS TO GEORGIA PASS
THE JEFFERSON TRAIL

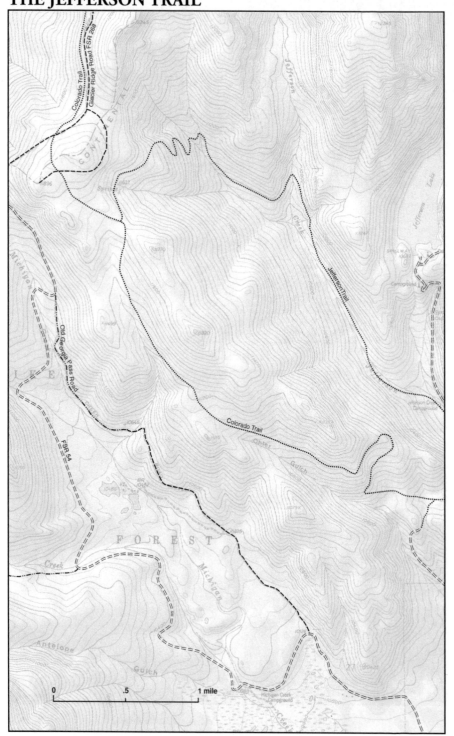

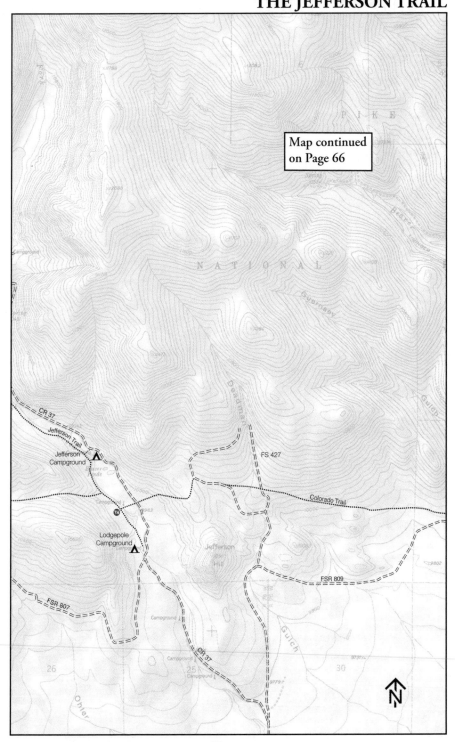

Map continued
on Page 66

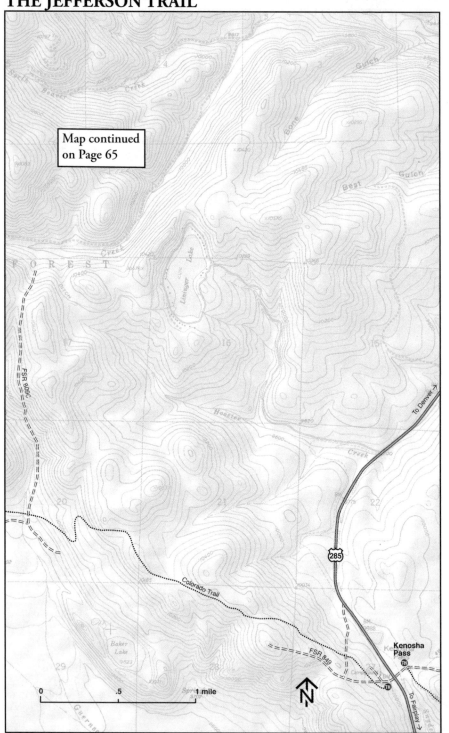

Map continued
on Page 65

THE COLORADO TRAIL
Kenosha Pass to Jefferson Trail
Ride Information

Description: This is a smooth, all singletrack ride, just 60 miles from Denver on Highway 285. The Colorado Trail on the other side of the highway is also an awesome ride, see Colorado Trail: Kenosha Pass to Rock Creek, page 72. Huge stands of aspens make this a great fall ride. There is plenty of camping around this popular area, and places to stay in Fairplay. The beginning of the trail flows in and out of dense pine forests and beautiful South Park meadowlands. As it nears Georgia Pass, it climbs high alpine meadows to an amazing viewpoint above the Swan River Valley. The whole ride has a pristine feel to it. Intermediate riders can ride the first six miles as an out and back. The upper section to Georgia Pass can be ridden as an out and back, or combined with the Jefferson Trail as a loop. The trail is a mostly moderate grade, with the exception of a steeper section after six miles. The descent down the Jefferson Trail is a little more challenging and rugged, but also a great descent. Expect to see other users on the Colorado Trail, and hunters in the fall.

Distance: 12 to 26 miles, all singletrack, as an out and back on the Colorado Trail; 24.5 miles as a loop, all singletrack except one mile of dirt road, with the Jefferson Creek Trail.

Time: 2 hours as an out and back to County Road 37, 4-6 hours as an out and back to Georgia Pass or as a loop with the Jefferson Trail.

Overall Difficulty: Intermediate to Expert

Technical Skill: Intermediate with short expert sections

Aerobic Effort: Moderate in the first 6 miles, high beyond that.

Elevation: Top: 11,900' Gain: 3,550' As a 12 mile out and back: Top: 10,500' Gain: 1,650'

Season: Late June through early October

Usage: Moderate

Finding Route: Easy, the Colorado Trail is well marked and an easy to follow. Look for the small double peaked Colorado Trail symbols on the trees.

Location: Begin this ride on the west side of Highway 285 on Kenosha Pass, approximately 60 miles south of Denver and 20 miles north of Fairplay. There is parking on the west side of the highway at the trailhead and in the highway right-of-way, and also ¼ mile east of the highway. There are restrooms at the east trailhead and parking area.

Maps: Latitude 40 Summit County Colorado Trails

Mileage Log:

0.0 The signed Colorado Trail singletrack begins just to the left of the road to Kenosha Campground, right next to Highway 285.

0.1 Stay left as a singletrack spur leads right to the campground. Cross Forest Road 859 and continue on the singletrack. The trail climbs gradually.

THE COLORADO TRAIL
Kenosha Pass to Jefferson Trail
Ride Information

4.4   Cross a powerline.

0.7   Cross a doubletrack.

1.0   Top out.

2.0   Begin dropping into the grassy South Park.

3.0   Turn left on Forest Road 809C, and immediately right on the singletrack. Next cross a bridge over Guernsey Creek, and ride straight ahead past side spurs.

4.5   Cross Forest Road 427.

4.6   Cross Deadman Creek.

5.4   Ride through a gate and descend.

6.1   Cross County Road 37. The singletrack continues straight ahead. (For an easier ride, this is a good spot to turn around.)

6.2   Cross Jefferson Creek.

6.3   Turn right at the trail intersection. (The Jefferson Trail continues left to the Lodgepole Campground.)

6.4   Turn left on the Colorado Trail to Georgia Pass. (Straight ahead goes to the Jefferson Campground.) The climbing becomes steeper and more technical from here.

8.1   Continue straight passing a spur leading to Michigan Creek Road that turns sharp left.

8.6   The trail continues past a rock outrcropping, and then levels.

6.6   Cross a creek.

11.0   Ride through beautiful open meadows as you approach tree line.

11.6   Arrive at the junction with the Jefferson Creek Trail. Turn here to make a loop, after a quick out and back to the pass for a view. For the view, continue left on the Colorado Trail (CT.)

12.0   Cross a road and continue straight up.

12.2   Arrive at the saddle for a great view. Return to the junction with the Jefferson Trail.

12.8   Here you have two choices: return as you came up on the CT, or take the Jefferson Trail to the left, as described here. Begin the Jefferson Trail by contouring around a big bowl, then descending tight switchbacks.

14.5   Cross a creek. The trail becomes easier and meanders down the creek.

15.3   Cross another creek.

16.5   Cross Jefferson Creek on a good bridge. The trail becomes rocky, then widens to a doubletrack.

17.5   End of the trail in the Jefferson Campground. Turn left and ride out toward County Road 37.

THE COLORADO TRAIL
Kenosha Pass to Jefferson Trail
Ride Information

17.6   Turn right on County Road 37.

18.4   Turn left and climb on the Colorado Trail. Don't miss this turn! Return the way you rode out.

24.5   Back to Kenosha Pass. 🚲

Nottingham Ridge Trail, Vail

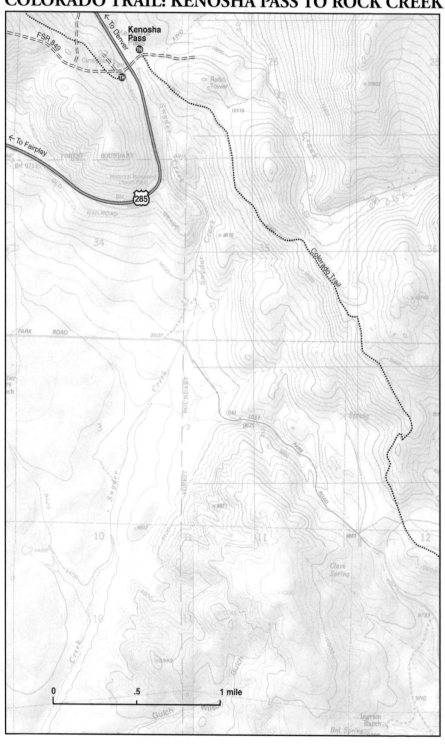

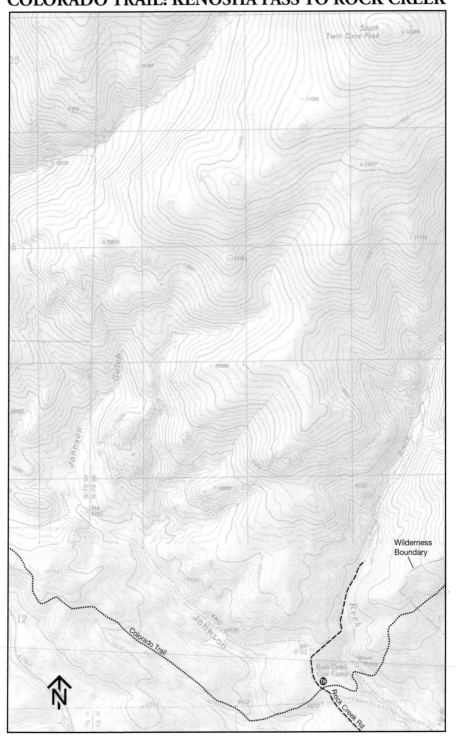

THE COLORADO TRAIL
Kenosha Pass to Rock Creek
Ride Information ───────────────────────────

Description:

This is a beautiful out and back on the Colorado Trail through open meadows and mixed stands of pine and aspens. Riders enjoy great views of The South Park and very fast singletrack. With the exception of a short rocky section near the trailhead, it is all smooth, mostly gradual singletrack. This is a popular area in the fall because of all the beautiful aspen colors. Be sure to wear orange during hunting season and use extra caution. Do not ride into the Lost Creek Wilderness, as this is illegal and carries a heavy fine, and your bike can be confiscated.

Distance: 13 miles out and back, all singletrack.

Time: 1 ½ – 2 ½ hours

Overall Difficulty: Intermediate

Technical Skill: Intermediate

Aerobic Effort: Moderate

Elevation: Top: 10,400' Gain:1,600'

Season: Late June through October

Usage: Moderate

Finding Route: Easy, the Colorado Trail is well marked and obvious. Look for the small double peaked Colorado Trail symbols on the trees.

Location: Begin this ride on the east side of Highway 285 on Kenosha Pass, approximately 60 miles south of Denver and 20 miles north of Fairplay. There is a parking lot and restrooms at the east trailhead, ¼ mile east of the highway.

Maps: National Geographic Trails Illustrated Tarryall Mountains-Kenosha Pass

Mileage Log:

0.0 Begin riding the smooth Colorado Trail just to the south of the parking area and restrooms.

0.2 Ride through a gate and climb gradually.

2.7 Awesome view of the South Park and surrounding mountains. Begin a nice descent through open, grassy meadows.

3.6 Continue on singletrack, straight across a doubletrack.

5.7 Pass a doubletrack spur on right.

6.0 Cross a small bridge over Johnson Gulch and climb again.

6.5 Arrive at Rock Creek Road 133. There is a trailhead sign here. Return the way you came.

13.0 Back to the trailhead and your car! 🚲

Colorado Trail: Kokomo Pass

Colorado Trail: Kokomo Pass

THE GOLD DUST TRAIL

THE GOLD DUST TRAIL

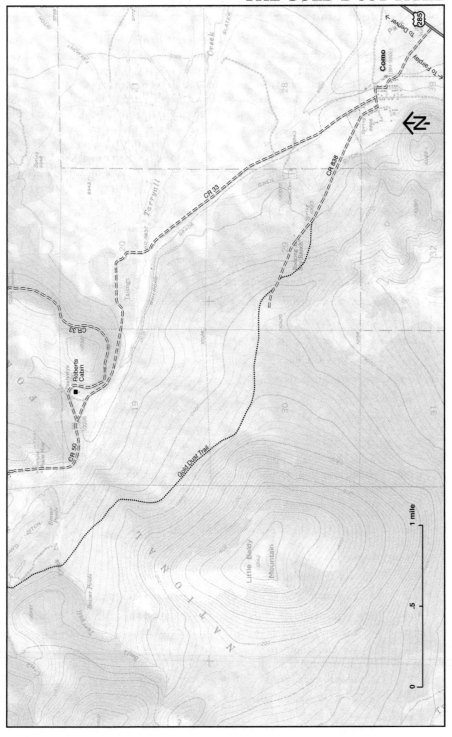

THE GOLD DUST TRAIL
Ride Information

Description: The Gold Dust Trail is a beautiful ride starting in the sleepy little town of Como, 9 miles north of Fairplay or 70 miles south of Denver on Highway 285. The loop meanders through and above the South Park, offering great views of Mount Guyot and Boreas Mountain. It begins with a scenic road ride and an easy flume trail that winds through the dense forest. Beginners can enjoy this first half of the ride (see option) while more advanced riders will enjoy the entire loop. The second half of the ride is intermediate singletrack through dark forest and aspen groves, covering a variety of terrain from smooth to rocky. This is a quiet break from busy trails, it is likely you'll have the trail to yourself. It is also good ridden in the opposite direction. After the ride, stop at the Como Depot Restaurant for a blast of history and a good old fashioned, home cooked meal.

Distance: Beginner loop: 10.4 mile loop, 7.6 miles of dirt road and 2.8 miles of singletrack. Intermediate loop: 17.5 mile loop, 9.2 miles of dirt road, 8.3 miles of singletrack.

Time: Beginner loop: 1-1 ½ hours; Intermediate loop: 2 ¼ -3 ¼ hours.

Overall Difficulty: Beginner to intermediate

Technical Skill: Beginner for the first half, intermediate for the second half.

Aerobic Effort: Moderate

Elevation: Beginner Loop: Top:10,650' Gain: 1,100'

Intermediate loop: Top: 10,650 Gain: 1,750'

Season: June through October

Usage: Light

Finding route: Moderate

Location: Drive 9 miles north of Fairplay on Colorado Highway 285 and turn left on County Road 33. Drive ½ mile toward Como and park on the right at the historic Como Roundhouse Train Depot or further in town for the intermediate loop. For the beginner loop, drive 3.2 miles farther on CR 33 and park at Roberts Cabin, at the junction of County Roads 33 and 50.

Maps: Latitude 40 Summit County Colorado Trails

Mileage Log:

0.0   Begin riding west through Como on County Road 33.

0.2   Continue straight on CR 33 when County Road 836 turns left.

0.4   The pavement ends. Continue on the gradual graded road.

3.2   Turn right at the fork in the road at Robert's Cabin, staying on County Road 33, and climb gradually toward Boreas Pass. Enjoy views of the Tarryall Mountains and Kenosha Pass from this road. (Park here at Robert's Cabin for the beginner version of the loop, see option.)

5.9   Pass the Rocky Point Trail on the left.

6.5   Turn left at the road junction toward the Selkirk Campground and North Tarryall Creek. Right continues to Boreas Pass.

7.7   Stay right, merging onto the incoming Forest Road 801.

7.8   Ride straight ahead on Forest Road 801, passing a spur to The Selkirk Campground on the right.

9.2   Turn left onto the hidden Gold Dust Trail, marked only with a small sign of a skier and a blue diamond on a tree. An old doubletrack turns off right, directly across from this trail. If you arrive at a creek crossing in a meadow and a fork in the road, you have gone 3/10ths of a mile too far.

9.4   Cross North Tarryall Creek. Roll along on this level ditch trail with fun banked corners, mainly in the dark forest.

10.3   Stay on the ditch trail as a faint spur takes off left.

11.4   The ditch is blocked off, turn left and descend.

12.0   Ride past a house on the left and arrive on County Road 50. Beginners turn left here and return to your vehicle. To continue on the trail, ride straight across the road and walk down the bank on the other side, onto the unmarked and obscure continuation of the trail. Just a little farther and to the left, the trail becomes more visible. Look for the "Danger, Thin Ice" signs. Cross a series of beam bridges over the wetlands, and climb the creek bank on the other side, following the blue diamonds into the forest.

12.1   Switchback up the hillside out of the creek. Soon begin a steady climb through the woods.

13.6   Fun rocky section!

14.7   Start descending through tight trees, following orange diamonds.

15.4   Stay left, passing a spur to the right.

15.8   Merge onto a road and descend. Continue following orange diamonds.

16.0   Turn right off the road at a fenced in area, and continue on the singletrack.

16.2   Ride through a gate.

16.5   Caution, a big drop onto CR 836! Camp Como is to the left. Turn right and descend back to the valley.

17.1   Back to Como.

17.3   Turn left on the first dirt road, then right on the paved CR 33 and return to your car.

17.6   Back to your car!

Option: For the beginner loop, drive 3.2 miles past the Roundhouse Historic Depot on CR 33 to Roberts Cabin. Park here. Turn right at the fork at Robert's Cabin, staying on CR 33. Follow the above directions from mile 3.2 to mile 12. Turn left on CR50 and return to your car. 🚲

THE AQUEDUCT TRAIL
KEYSTONE GULCH TO WEST RIDGE

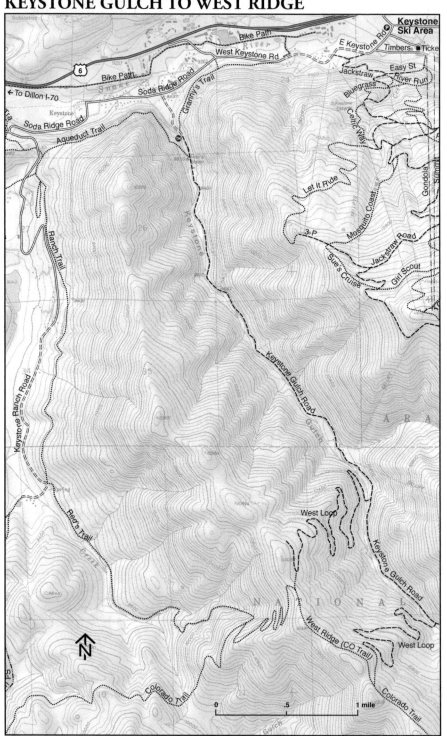

THE AQUEDUCT TRAIL

Ride Information

Description:

The Aqueduct Trail combined with Soda Ridge Road is a good beginner loop. It is flat and wide, and also a scenic ride. There are several possibilities to lengthen the ride, see option. Expect to see other users on this loop, and always yield to horses.

Distance: 3.3 mile loop, 1.5 miles of paved road, .3 of dirt road, 1.5 miles of singletrack. Time: 45 minutes, add up to 2 hours with the addition of Keystone Ranch Road or Keystone Gulch Road.

Overall Difficulty: Beginner

Technical Skill: Beginner

Aerobic Effort: Low

Elevation: Top: 9,400' Gain: 350'. Add up to 600' on Keystone Gulch Road.

Season: June through October

Finding Route: Easy

Maps: Latitude 40 Summit County Colorado Trails

Location: Park at the Keystone Gulch Trailhead. To get here from I70, take exit 205 to Keystone Ski Area and stay on Highway 6 for 6 ½ miles. Turn right on West Keystone Road. Turn immediately left and descend to cross the creek, then turn right on Soda Ridge Road. Drive ½ mile to Keystone Gulch Road, and turn left. Just 1/10th of a mile up is the trailhead and parking. Park Here. To ride here from the Keystone Ski Area Base, ride west on West Keystone Road and then Soda Ridge Road; or take the intermediate Granny's Trail, which starts 2/10ths of a mile from the western parking lots at Keystone. This leads right to the trailhead. The trailhead is a little over 1 mile from the parking lots.

Mileage Log:

0.0   Ride down Keystone Gulch Road to Soda Ridge Road and turn left.

0.6   Turn left at a sign for the Keystone stables and begin climbing gradually, now on Keystone Ranch Road.

1.3   Cross a singletrack, still on the paved road.

1.5   Turn left onto the singletrack marked by large rocks directly across from the signed Rossater Trail. Pass a singletrack that turns right and parallels the road. Ride up the hill and turn left on The Aqueduct Trail. (Or continue out Keystone Ranch Road for a longer ride, see option.)

1.6   Pass a singletrack to the left and stay right along the ditch.

2.2   Stay right along the ditch as a steep trail to the left descends to a neighborhood.

2.5   Caution! Walk your bike along the culverts and board planks.

2.9   Ride up Keystone Creek, passing spurs to the left.

3.0   Turn left and cross Keystone Creek on a doubletrack. To return to your car, turn left and ride down the road. Not enough riding yet? Turn right and

79

ride up Keystone Gulch Road as far as you like and then return the way you came up.

3.3 Back to your car, or ride back to Keystone on Granny's Trail, to the right.

Option: Continue out Keystone Ranch Road about 2 ½ miles until just before the road descends to an old homestead. Here you have several options. Turn left onto the singletrack, and turn left to head back to the Aqueduct Trail. This is the intermediate Ranch Trail. OR turn right and enjoy the quiet and scenic 1 ½ mile beginner section of Red's Trail. Ride as far as you like, and then return the way you came. OR stay right on the road and descend to the homestead. On the right is an unmarked singletrack that heads up Soda Creek. This trail starts out easy, and then branches off into more difficult sections. See Rossater and West Ranch Trails, page 85, for more information on this area. 🚲

THE COLORADO TRAIL
Keystone Gulch to West Ridge
Ride Information ———————————— *See map page 78*

Description:

The West Ridge section of The Colorado Trail is fast, fun, and smooth, rolling in and out of drainages and over small hills. The access up Keystone Gulch Road is a gradual 45 minute spin, and the climb to the West Ridge is more moderate and gradual than is the Colorado Trail from The North Fork of the Swan Road on the Breckenridge side. The descent on the Red and Aqueduct Trails are smooth and fast, a great way to finish off the loop. This is one of the best!

Distance: 17.6 mile loop, 6.6 miles of dirt road and 11 miles of singletrack.

Time: 2-3 hours

Overall Difficulty: Intermediate

Technical Skill: Intermediate

Aerobic Effort: Moderate

Elevation: Top: 11,200' Gain: 2,200'

Season: Mid-June to early October

Usage: Moderate

Finding Route: Moderate

Maps: Latitude 40 Summit County Colorado Trails or Sky Terrain Summit, Vail & Holy Cross

Location: To get to the Keystone Gulch Trailhead from I70, take exit 205 to Keystone Ski Area and stay on Highway 6 for 6 1/2 miles. Turn right on West Keystone Road, then immediately left and descend to cross the creek. Turn right on Soda Ridge Road.

THE COLORADO TRAIL
Keystone Gulch to West Ridge

—— Ride Information

Drive 1/2 mile to Keystone Gulch Road, and turn left. The trailhead is 1/10th of a mile up. Park here. To ride from the Keystone Ski Area Base, head west from the western parking lots on West Keystone Road and then Soda Ridge Road, or take Granny's Trail, which starts 2/10ths of a mile from the parking lot and ends at the trailhead. It is 1.3 miles from the parking lot to the trailhead.

Mileage Log:

0.0 Begin riding up Keystone Gulch Road. You will stay on this road for 4.4 miles.

3.2 Continue straight on Keystone Gulch Road, passing the signed lower turn to the West Loop on the right.

4.2 Pass the Outback Express lift on the right.

4.4 Turn right on the signed West Ridge Loop dirt road. As you follow this route, look for the red signs with a bike symbol, and also blue arrows. Some of the signs are in disrepair or missing.

4.7 The road forks, turn right and descend off the ski area access road. Cross the creek and climb for ¾ mile. The road levels and then descends to the next fork.

5.9 Turn left at this next fork, and climb a rocky hill.

6.0 Climb steeply for a short distance to the next fork, and turn right.

6.1 Keep left and ride up around the switchback at the next fork.

6.3 Ride straight ahead, passing a sharp cutback to the right of an old unused trail. Climb briefly to a long straightaway.

6.7 Turn sharp right on The Colorado Trail. Look for the double peaked CT symbols.

7.7 Begin the long fast downhill!

7.9 Stay left on the Colorado Trail. Right descends to Keystone Gulch Road via the Lower West Loop, also old doubletrack.

10.2 Ride straight ahead onto Red's Trail when the Colorado Trail cuts sharp left in the sage meadow.

10.7 Ride left or right, the trail rejoins. Descend through the dark forest.

13.2 Intersection with Keystone Ranch Road. Turn right, staying on the Ranch Trail singletrack.

14.8 Stay right on the singletrack next to a paved road.

15.0 Cross Wild Iris Lane, and continue on the ditchbank singletrack.

15.2 Cross a paved road and continue following the ditch.

15.5 Ride straight ahead on an old doubletrack and pass singletrack spurs to the left and right. Climb gradually through an old gate.

15.7 Pass a singletrack coming in from the left.

THE COLORADO TRAIL
Keystone Gulch to West Ridge
Ride Information

15.8 Stay right, passing a spur on the left.

15.9 Stay right along the ditch on the Aqueduct Trail. Watch for other users on this section.

16.5 Stay right passing a steep descending trail to the left.

16.8 Caution! I suggest walking over the culverts and board planks.

17.2 Stay right and ride up Keystone Creek.

17.3 Turn left and cross Keystone Creek to Keystone Gulch Road. Turn left and descend.

17.6 Back to the parking lot! 🚲

Red's Trail, off the Colorado Trail

Red's Trail

ROSSATER & WEST RANCH TRAILS

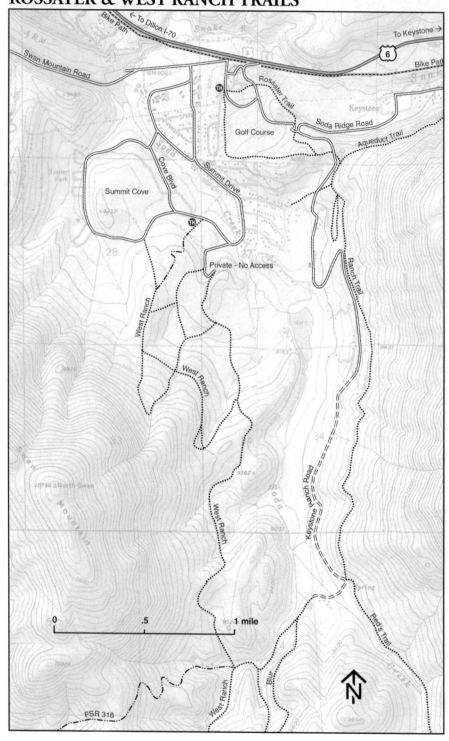

ROSSATER & WEST RANCH TRAILS

Ride Information

Description:

This combination of smooth, fun trails just outside of Keystone is a perfect afternoon ride. The non-motorized loop rolls through dense conifer forests, aspen groves, and beautiful meadows. The climbs are gradual, and the descents fast and smooth. This area has plenty of other great singletracks to explore with the Latitude 40 Summit County Trails and Sky Terrain Summit, Vail, Holy Cross maps. Don't miss riding in this wonderful area of singletracks!

Distance: 9 mile loop, 6 miles of singletrack, 2 miles paved road, 1 mile of doubletrack.

Time: 1½-2 hours

Overall Difficulty: Intermediate

Technical Skill: Intermediate

Aerobic Effort: Moderate

Elevation: Top: 9,550' Gain: 1,050'

Season: Late May through mid October

Usage: Moderate

Finding Route: Moderate in the beginning of the loop, difficult toward the end of the loop. There are many turns and spurs, and most are not marked. It can be confusing navigating through neighborhood trail systems near the Summit Cove subdivision. However, if you do get off the main loop, most trails lead to the subdivision and it is fairly straightforward to return through the subdivision to the Soda Ridge Trailhead.

Location: Start at the Soda Ridge Trailhead. To get here, drive approximately 3 ½ miles south of Dillon or 4 ½ miles south of I70 on Highway 6 toward Keystone. Just past the resevoir, turn right on Swan Mountain Road. Turn immediately left and travel 6/10ths of a mile to the end of Soda Springs Road to the Soda Ridge Trailhead. Park here. For other access points and parking, see option.

Maps: Latitude 40 Summit County Colorado Trails is best, or Sky Terrain Summit, Vail, Holy Cross.

Mileage Log:

0.0   Ride through the gate in the parking area fence and turn left onto the paved and signed Community Path to Snake River Pathway. Follow this up toward the golf course.

0.2   Stay left at the fork in the paved path.

0.3   Cross a road intersection below the clubhouse, traveling straight ahead from the paved path, and look for the singletrack that begins to the right. There is a green sign "Rossater Trail." Follow this trail up behind the clubhouse.

0.5   Cross a golf cart path.

0.8   Ride straight ahead and continue climbing. (To the right returns to the Soda

ROSSATER & WEST RANCH TRAILS
Ride Information

Ridge Trailhead via Idlewild Drive.)

1.0   Cross the paved Keystone Ranch Road and turn immediately right on the lower singletrack. Large rocks mark the trail entrance. Climb gently alongside the road. Continue straight ahead as The Aqueduct Trail merges in from the left. Spin along the old road grade.

1.2   Stay left when a singletrack descends to the right.

1.3   Arrive at a 5-way intersection by an old gate. Ride straight ahead taking the most prominent trail to the left, and staying on a level grade (Not the sharp, steep left.)

1.5   Roll onto a ditchbank.

1.8   Descend and cross Iris Lane. Continue on the singletrack.

2.1   Continue on the singletrack, climbing into the forest.

3.6   Stay right and descend toward Keystone Ranch Road. Turn left on the road and ride toward the ranch buildings. (The Red's singletrack continues left toward the Colorado Trail. Also an excellent ride.)

3.8   Turn right on an unmarked singletrack below the ranch buildings, and cross an old dam.

3.9   Stay right at a fork and roll along this flat, smooth section. (Left is the Blur Trail and climbs, leading to the Horseshoe Gulch Trail, FS 351.)

4.4   Stay right at another fork. (Left is quite steep and also climbs to FS 351.)

4.6   Turn right at another fork and cross a small creek, climbing through beautiful meadows. (Left heads toward the powerlines and the Colorado Trail, where a right leads to the Gold Hill Trailhead.)

5.9   Arrive at a spur, turn left and climb on the more prominent trail.

6.0   Stay right at the fork. The left fork rejoins in 1/10th of a mile. Climb and descend a short, steep hill.

6.2   Views of big open meadows and the golf course in the Soda Creek drainage.

6.9   Ride through an old pole fence, cross a singletrack and continue straight ahead. There is an immediate split, stay right. (If you lose the loop at this point or beyond, you will end in the Summit Cove subdivision. Be sure to turn right on Cove Boulevard or Summit Drive and head back to Soda Ridge Road. These two roads form the main loop of the Summit Cove subdivision.)

7.1   Cross over a singletrack.

7.3   Turn right just before entering a sage meadow, and descend on a doubletrack.

7.4   The road forks. Turn left, then turn immediately right and down when the road forks again.

7.6   Split left onto a singletrack, then as it forks, turn right and down a switchback and straight into a neightborhood.

7.7   Enter the parking area through the fence opening and turn right on Summit

Drive. Continue on this road to Swan Mountain Road.

8.9 (approx. mileage) Turn right on Swan Mountain Road.

9.1 Turn right on Soda Springs Road, just before Highway 6, and follow this around and up to the Soda Ridge Trailhead.

9.5 End at your car.

Option: To access the Soda Creek Trails from Keystone Gulch Trailhead (west of Keystone off Soda Ridge Road,) ride west on Soda Ridge Road and turn left at the stables sign in 6/10ths of a mile. Continue on Keystone Ranch Road 9/10ths mile to where the Rossater Trail crosses the road. It is marked with large rocks. Also see The Colorado Trail: Keystone Gulch to the West Ridge and the Aqueduct Trail, page 80, for a more challenging ride that ends in this area, or Aqueduct Trail, page 79, for a beginner ride in this area.

To access the Soda Creek Trails from Breckenridge, see Horseshoe Gulch to the Colorado Trail, page 50. Another access option is from the Gold Hill Trailhead between Frisco and Breckenridge. See Colorado Trail, Middle Fork, page 51. From here, ride south toward Breckenridge and turn left off the paved bike path in 2/10ths of a mile. The Colorado Trail begins up Revette Road. The very steep FS 316 begins off this road, also. See the Latitude 40 map for details. ⚧

Paid in Full, Keystone Ski Area

KEYSTONE SKI AREA

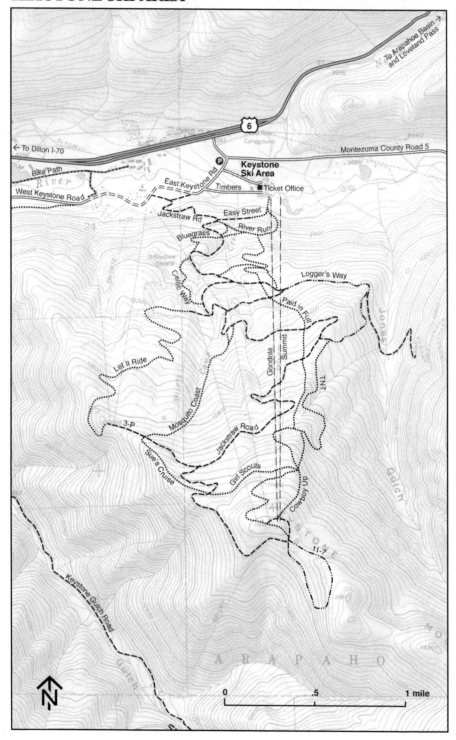

KEYSTONE CROSS COUNTRY LOOPS

Keystone offers a variety of loops for the cross country rider. There are two ways to ride up, on Jackstraw Road or by linking the "green" rated or easy singletracks. These trails are a gradual, pleasant ride up and no more difficult than Jackstraw Road. These same easy trails are the best way down for those who enjoy fast and smooth singletrack. The "blue" rated or moderate trails are very rough from heavy downhill use, but still fun for a cross country mountain biker. A couple of the black trails are good for expert cross country riders, while the double blacks are for downhillers only. Neither the blue or black trails are good uphill trails. See Keystone Downhill Trails, page 92, for more information. The ski area is well marked during the summer season which starts mid- June, depending on snow, and runs through Labor Day weekend. If you want to ride downhill only, tickets are available at the ticket office at the base area, near the pedestrian bridge by the lifts. When riding up or when riding at a moderate pace downhill, be sure to watch for high speed downhillers coming up on you or at intersections.

Loop 1: Let it Ride to Mosquito Coast

Description:

This is a fun out and back on the easier trails, or loop linking the easier trails with a challenging but fast descent. If you enjoy a fast, smooth descent, descend the way you ride up. The descent for the loop starts with The Mosquito Coast Trail, a bumpy and rocky but fast downhill. If you prefer to ride up the road, see option.

Distance: 9.2 mile loop, mostly singletrack

Time: 1-1 ½ hours

Overall Difficulty: Intermediate if you descend the "Green Trails." Advanced Intermediate to Expert if you descend Mosquito Coast and River Run. These trails are quite rocky and rooted.

Technical Skill: Intermediate to Expert

Aerobic Effort: Moderate

Elevation: Top: 10,950' Gain: 1,600'

Season: June through early October

Usage: Light to moderate; moderate to heavy on weekends when lifts are running.

Finding Route: Easy to moderate. There are many turns, but the trails are well marked during the summer season and flow quite well into one another. For most of the ride, just follow the route up.

Location: Start at the base of the Summit Express lift. This is located just across the pedestrian bridge from the ticket windows at the Keystone Ski Area Base. Keystone is located about 7 miles from I70 exit 205 on Highway 6. Turn right on East Keystone Road and park on the right. Turn left on River Run Road to get to the ticket office and bridge to the trails.

KEYSTONE CROSS COUNTRY LOOPS
Ride Information

Maps: Keystone Bike Park Map, available at the base area.

Mileage Log:

0.0 Ride up and left toward the lift line from the pedestrian bridge. Turn right at the fork on Easy Street.

0.2 The trail forks again. Turn right and cross a large bridge and climb up the doubletrack.

0.4 Turn left on Jackstraw Road and ride up the first switchback.

0.5 Turn left on the Sleepyhollow singletrack.

0.9 The trail forks, turn right and up toward Jackstraw Road.

1.0 Cross Jackstraw Road and ride straight onto the Bluegrass singletrack.

1.3 Stay right, passing a spur to the left that leads to Jackstraw Road.

1.5 Stay right passing a spur to the left that leads to Jackstraw Road. Begin the Celtic Way Singletrack.

1.9 Cross a closed road.

2.1 Turn right and climb on Jackstraw Road.

2.2 Turn right at the fork in the road onto Let it Ride, a doubletrack. Just to the left of this turn are ski area buildings.

2.3 Turn right as Let It Ride forks off into a singletrack.

2.7 Cross a doubletrack and continue on the singletrack into the woods.

4.3 Cross a service road, stay on the singletrack.

4.9 Cross another service road.

5.2 Ride straight ahead onto the 3-P Road and climb. This is where you turn around to return down the green trails. If you want to continue to the Summit, take 3-P to Jackstraw and turn right. At the top descend via Girl Scouts and Suz's Cruz back to here.

5.3 Turn left and descend on the Mosquito Coast Trail. This is a washboarded, rocky, and rooted descent.

6.2 Stay left or take the jumps to the right!

6.6 Stay left at the fork.

6.7 Turn left onto Jackstraw Road and descend.

6.8 Pass a singletrack on the right. Stay on the road.

6.9 Pass the Ride On singletrack on the right of a switchback.

7.1 Turn left onto the Celtic Way Singletrack.

7.3 Cross a doubletrack.

7.8 Stay left on the Bluegrass singletrack.

7.9 Stay left on the singletrack.

8.3 Cross Jackstraw Road and continue on the Sleepyhollow singletrack. Stay left at the next fork on Sleepyhollow.

8.8   Turn right on Jackstraw Road.

8.9   Turn right on Easy Street.

9.1   Take any trail back to the base of lift.

Option: To ride up Jackstraw Road, follow the directions in Loop 2, below, to mile 4.4. Turn right on 3-P Road. Continue about ½ mile to the Mosquito Coast Trail on the right, or 1/10th of a mile farther to the smoother Let It Ride.

Loop 2: Jackstraw Road to TNT and Loggers Way

Description:

Jackstraw Road is a gradual way to reach the summit of the ski area. Riding down TNT and Loggers Way are challenging, steep descents. They are rough old two-tracks, but very fast and fun.

Distance: 11.6 mile loop, 6 miles dirt road, 5.6 miles of singletrack and old road.

Time: 1 ½-2 hours

Overall Difficulty: Expert

Technical Skill: Expert

Aerobic Effort: Moderate

Elevation: Top: 11,640' Gain: 2,350'

Season: June through early October

Usage: Light to moderate, moderate to heavy on weekends when lifts are running.

Finding Route: Easy

Location: Start at the Keystone Medical Center. To get here from the ticket office (see location, Loop 1, above) cross the pedestrian bridge and turn right on the Timbers Trail. Follow this until it ends on Trailhead Road. Ride 2/10ths of a mile and turn left on East Keystone Road. The medical center is on the left, ¼ mile from Trailhead Road. Or, from the parking area, turn right and follow East Keystone Road to the medical center.

Mileage:

0.0   Ride to the left of the medical center and climb Jackstraw Road.

0.3   Stay right passing Easy Street Road on the left.

1.2   Stay right at the fork in the road. Cadillac Road is the left fork.

1.6   Stay left at the fork, passing the Let it Ride doubletrack on right.

4.4   Stay left at fork in the road. 3-P Road is the right turn.

4.8   Pass Girl Scouts and Suz's Cruz singletracks. (Girl Scouts to the left also leads to TNT. See map.)

5.7   Continue straight ahead, passing the 11-7 road on the right.

5.9   Pass Cowboy Up on the right and ride under the lift lines.

KEYSTONE CROSS COUNTRY LOOPS
Ride Information

6.1   (approx. mileage) Continue to the end of Jack Straw Road and ride onto Girl Scouts. Stay right.

7.1   Three-way intersection. Ride straight ahead onto on TNT.

7.4   Switchback to the right, passing a trail to the left.

8.4   Stay left passing Punk Rock to the right.

8.5   Punk Rock descends in on the right.

8.6   The trail forks immediately, turn right on Loggers Way.

9.7   Turn right onto Jaybird Road toward Boy Scouts, then left onto the singletrack.

10.0 Continue past two trails coming in on left.

10.1 Continue straight, passing Wild Thing to the right.

10.2 Turn right onto Jackstraw Road and descend.

10.5 Turn left onto Bluegrass, turn immediately right and descend.

10.7 Cross Jackstraw road and ride onto the Sleepyhollow singletrack.

10.8 Turn right on River Run.

11.3 Trails merge, ride straight ahead onto the doubletrack.

11.7 Turn right toward the base.

11.8 Back to base. 🚲

KEYSTONE DOWNHILL TRAILS
Ride Information

Keystone features more than two dozen downhill trails accessed by the Summit express chairlift. There are trails for every level of rider from beginner to expert. The expert (black) downhill trails are the longest, most technical downhill courses in the nation. Keystone recommends downhill bikes and gear for these technical courses. All trails start and end at the base of the Summit Express lift. This is located just across the pedestrian bridge from the ticket office at the Keystone Ski Area Base. Keystone is located about 7 miles from I70 exit 205 on Highway 6. Turn right on East Keystone Road and park on the right. Turn left on River Run Road to get to the ticket office and bridge to the trails.

Easy and intermediate trails:

Jackstraw Road: A gradual road to the top of the mountain. Easy descent.
Girl Scouts, Suz's Cruz, Let it Ride, Celtic Way, Bluegrass, Sleepy Hollow, and ***Easy Street:*** These trails are the best cross country routes. They are smooth, fast singletracks, easily linked for a high speed descent. Combined, they are also a great uphill route to the summit of the mountain. They wind through the forest and switchback down ski runs. Quite fun! Watch for uphill riders if you are descending them. These trails are lightly used. See Loop 1, page 89, for details.

Granny's Trail: A short intermediate and technical trail that connects Keystone to Keystone Gulch. Located 2/10ths of a mile west of the western Keystone parking areas.

Advanced intermediate to expert trails:

Mosquito Coast, River Run Trail, Loggers Way, TNT: These trails are fine for advanced cross country riders. They are steep and fast, but rough and heavily used. Lots of roots and rocks. Watch for high speed downhillers on these trails. These are not suitable for uphill riding.

Mosquito Coast: A fast trail that winds through the woods off 3-P Road. Roots and rocks.

TNT and Loggers Way: Especially fast old doubletrack and singletrack with long straightaways.

River Run Trail: Short trail to the base area, heavily used. High speed straightaways and fairly large ruts and drops.

Decatur practice park (located near Lakeside Village): Beginner park with berms, whoopdy-dos and log rides.

Expert downhill trails:

Cowboy Up: a gnarly short trail featuring tight technical turns, log drops and a huge rock garden.

Punk Rock: a short technnical singletrack across a boulder field.

Motorhead: singletrack with berms, step downs, table tops, bridges and rocky descents.

Wild Thing: a very technical, narrow singletrack with tight turns, twists and massive rock drops.

Paid in Full: this new trail opened in 2004. Features table tops, a banked wooden flume, tall bridges, and steep drops. You must be an excellent technical rider with great balance! The bridges are very committing and narrow.

ASX Skill Park: At the base of the Summit Express lift, all kinds of constantly changing freeride terrain.

Discovery 4-cross course: Advanced Freeride Park at the base of the mountain. 🚲

photo by Jack Affleck

Keystone Ski Area: Loggers Way

COPPER MOUNTAIN SKI AREA

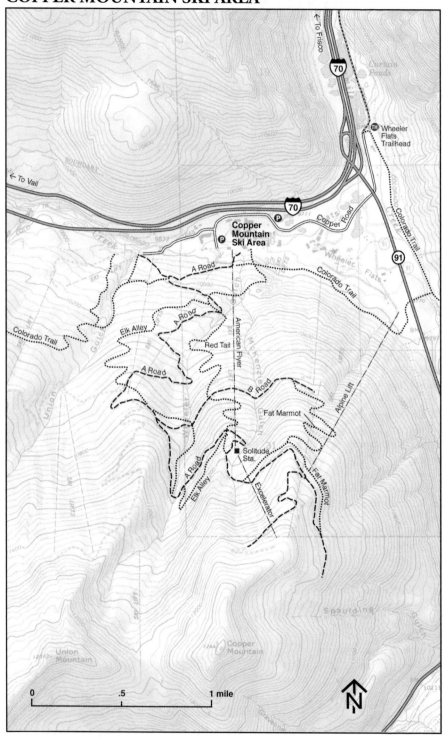

COPPER MOUNTAIN SKI AREA
Ride Information

The Copper Mountain Ski Area trails are built for cross country mountain biking, with fun, banked corners and just the right pitch. Designs are in the works for new trails here, as well. These trails stay away from the ski runs and lifts, so riders have a feeling of being out in the woods, not at a ski area. During the summer season, which lasts from late June (depending on snow) to Labor Day, the trails are well marked. Tickets are available at the Mountain Adventure Center at the Copper Mountain Base Area if you would like to ride downhill only. The A Road, The Redtail Trail and The Elk Alley Trail are also moderate uphill trails. The top section of the Fat Marmot Trail is a good uphill trail, but below Solitude Station it is better as a descent. It is easy to connect several loops in one day.

Description:

Both the Elk Alley and Redtail (see option 1) trails are moderate, intermediate singletracks with a lot of fun, smooth sections and banked corners. Follow the A Road up the mountain, an intermediate, gradual climb. The Fat Marmot Trail (see option 2) is rated intermediate above Solitude Station, but below, this switchbacking trail is more advanced.

Distance: Elk Alley: 8.6 mile loop, 4 miles of dirt road, 4.6 miles of singletrack. Redtail: 8.3 mile loop, 4 miles of dirt road, 4.6 miles of singletrack. Add 4 miles for the Fat Marmot Trail, 2 miles of road, 2 miles of singletrack.

Time: 1-3 hours, depending on loop.

Overall Difficulty: Intermediate

Technical Skill: Intermediate with a few advanced intermediate sections.

Aerobic Effort: Moderate

Elevation: Top: 11,200' Gain:1,600'. Combined with the Fat Marmot Trail: Top: 11,500' Gain: 2,000'

Season: June through early October

Usage: Light

Finding Route: Easy

Location: Exit Interstate 70 at Copper Mountain, 5 ½ miles west of Frisco, onto Highway 91 toward Leadville. Turn right on Copper Road and continue about 2 miles to the Copper Circle Parking Area, at the bottom of the American Flier Lift. The A road access to the top of Copper Mountain is to the left of the American Flier as you look up the mountain.

Maps: Copper Mountain summer trails map, available at the base area. Latitude 40 Summit County Trails.

Mileage Log:

0.0   Ride up and left on the access road just to the left of American Flier lift.

0.5   Turn left at the T intersection with A Road and climb. Right descends to Union Creek.

COPPER MOUNTAIN SKI AREA
Ride Information

0.7   Stay right and climb, passing a spur to the left.

1.1   Stay right on the main road, passing a spur to ski area maintenance buildings on the left.

2.1   Stay left and continue climbing on A Road.

2.4   Stay left at the fork, staying on A Road. There is a small building to the left here.

2.7   Arrive at a fork with B Road, turn right and continue climbing on A Road.

3.8   Turn right at the fork in the road at Solitude Station. The Excelerator lift is on the left. In less than $1/10^{th}$ of a mile, before you reach the top of another lift, is the beginning of the Redtail and Elk Alley trails on the right. Start down this smooth trail in the woods.

4.1   The trail splits just before A Road. Turn left onto the Elk Alley Trail. (See option 1 for the Red Tail Trail, right.) The Elk Alley trail climbs a bit and crosses some fun talus "bridges."

4.7   Turn left and ride down A Road briefly, and cross a creek.

4.8   Turn immediately right on the continuation of the singletrack just past the creek. It begins by the ski trails sign.

5.2   Pass a building and arrive on B Road. Turn left and climb the road very briefly to the continuation of the singletrack on the right.

5.3   Once on the trail again, stay left and climb, passing a closed singletrack on the right.

5.4   Turn right on A road.

5.5   Turn right on the hidden singletrack in the dark trees. If you come to a small building and road junction, you have gone too far and missed this turn.

5.7   Cross A Road and continue straight on the singletrack. Begin switchbacking down.

6.7   Stay on the trail.

7.3   Merge with the Red Tail singletrack under a lift. Turn left and descend on this fun, banked section of trail.

7.4   Cross the road and continue on the singletrack.

7.6   Stay right and descend the singletrack, passing a spur road that climbs to the left.

7.7   Stay left and contour on singletrack. A steep trail will cross the Elk Alley Trail several times more in the next 4/10ths of a mile, stay on the more gradual switchbacks.

8.2   Cross a creek.

8.5   Cross the Colorado Trail and descend to the base area.

8.6   Back to the base.

Option 1: Redtail Trail

0.0   Follow the above directions to mile 4.1.

COPPER MOUNTAIN SKI AREA

4.1 The trail splits just before reaching A Road. Turn right onto the Redtail Trail and immediately cross A Road. Enjoy this fast, smooth pine needle covered section.

5.3 Cross B Road.

6.5 Cross a bridge over a creek.

6.7 Cross a bridge over the creek.

7.0 Cross A Road. This section is fun, bermed singletrack.

7.1 Merge with the Elk Alley Trail. Turn right and continue down, under a lift.

7.2 Cross the road and continue on singletrack.

7.4 Stay right on the singletrack, passing a spur road that climbs to the left.

7.6 Stay left and contour on the singletrack. A steep trail will cross the Elk Alley Trail several times, but stay on the more gradual switchbacks.

8.0 Cross a bridge and creek.

8.3 Cross the Colorado Trail and descend to the base area.

8.4 Back to the base area.

Option 2:

Fat Marmot Trail

0.0 Follow the above directions to mile 3.8.

3.8 Turn right and continue climbing at the fork in the road at Solitude Station. Pass the beginning of the Elk Alley and Redtail Trails. Switchback up.

4.1 Continue up the road, passing the lower entrance to the Fat Marmot Trail.

4.7 The road forks just after going under the top of the Alpine Lift. Turn left onto the less prominent doubletrack.

4.9 As the road starts to descend slightly, turn left onto the Fat Marmot Trail, near the "To Super Bee Lift" ski sign. Nice views of the Ten Mile Range

5.2 Ride straight ahead on the singletrack, passing a spur to the left.

5.8 Pop out onto a run above Solitude Station. Turn sharp right at the fork. Have fun on this more challenging set of switchbacks!

6.9 Turn left on B Road at the end singletrack.

7.0 Stay on the main road.

7.4 Cross the Red Tail Trail. (Or take this to the bottom!)

7.8 Cross the Elk Alley Trail. (Or take this to the bottom!)

8.0 Turn sharp left on A road and climb to Solitude Station. Continue 1/10th farther to the turn for the Elk Alley and Red Tail Trails, and enjoy one of these singletracks down! 🚲

COLORADO TRAIL: SEARLE PASS

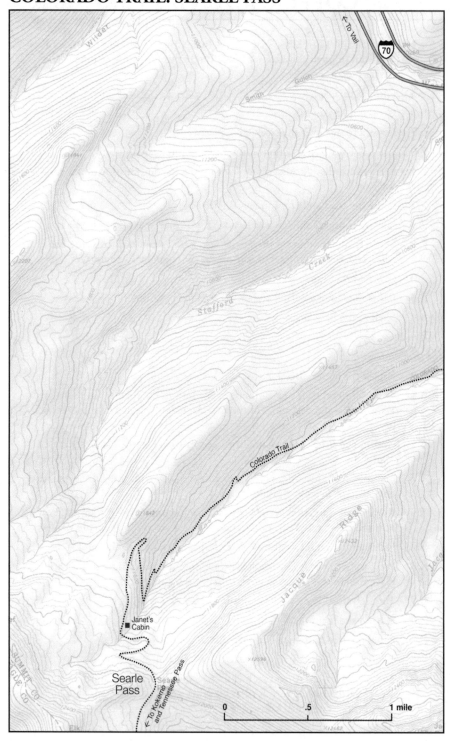

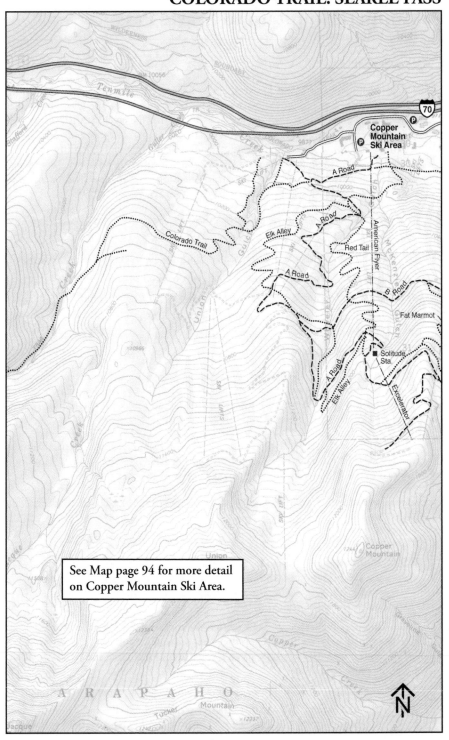

See Map page 94 for more detail on Copper Mountain Ski Area.

THE COLORADO TRAIL
Copper Mountain to Searle Pass
Ride Information

Description:

This awesome ride starts with a traverse across Copper Mountain Ski Area, and climbs into a beautiful high alpine valley, away from the roar of I70. The climb up Guller Creek is long and gradual, through lush meadows along the creek. Searle Pass rewards the rider with awesome views of the Ten Mile Range. The upper part of the ride requires strong fitness and good technical skills, but intermediate riders can enjoy the Guller Creek Valley and turn around at any point. The descent back to Copper is fast and smooth. This ride can be continued to Elk Ridge or Kokomo Pass, or down to Camp Hale and Tennessee Pass with a long shuttle. See option, below.

Distance: 22 mile out and back, all singletrack except ½ mile of dirt road!

Time: 3-5 hours

Overall Difficulty: Advanced Intermediate until mile 8.5, expert beyond this point.

Technical Skill: Advanced Intermediate- Expert beyond mile 8.5.

Aerobic Effort: Moderate-High beyond mile 8.5.

Elevation: Top: 12,040' Gain: 3,000' feet. Add 800 feet if ride is continued to Kokomo Pass and back.

Season: July through early October

Usage: Moderate

Finding Route: Moderate across the Copper Mountain Ski Area, easy after leaving the ski area. Always follow the main trail and look for the double-peaked Colorado Trail markers.

Location: From I70 take exit 195 to Copper Mountain and Leadville. Turn left almost immediately, just across from Copper Road and drive past the Copper Mountain Conoco to the Wheeler Flats Trailhead, at the end of the road. Park here.

Maps: Latitude 40 Summit County, Colorado Trails or the Sky Terrain Summit, Vail, Holy Cross

Mileage Log:

0.0   Ride out of the parking lot and onto the paved bike path toward Frisco. Cross a bridge and turn immediately right on an unmarked grassy two-track. Ride across a big cement bridge and follow the old railroad grade along Tenmile Creek.

1.0   Intersect the Colorado Trail. Turn right and cross a bridge, then turn immediately left and ride up the creek on an old doubletrack. Ride straight ahead for 1/10th of a mile passing spurs and campsites to the right. The road narrows to a singletrack.

1.4   Cross Highway 91 and ride back onto the singletrack. Begin switchbacking up.

2.5   The trail traverses above the golf greens, descends briefly, and continues to traverse above the condos. The trail turns to doubletrack.

3.1 Cross a creek and climb under a lift. Take the lower singletrack that climbs gradually across the ski run.

3.2 Merge onto a ski area access road, and continue climbing gradually.

3.6 At the next switchback, arrive at a road and trail intersection. There is a ski area sign here "To Union Creek." Ride straight across the road intersection and onto the singletrack, just to the left of the sign and the road to Union Creek. Look for the Colorado Trail symbol painted on a rock.

3.8 Turn left at the fork in the trail. There is a lot of horse traffic here, be cautious and always yield.

4.3 Turn left and climb at another fork in the trail.

4.4 Stay right and contour past a steep, rough trail on the left, next pass a closed trail on the right.

4.5 Stay left passing a steep spur on the right.

4.8 Turn right at the fork, staying with the Colorado Trail. Straight ahead is a rougher horse trail.

5.0 Cross ski runs and then traverse into the woods, leaving the ski area.

6.1 Ride straight ahead at the intersection, passing a spur to the left.

6.4 Cross a bridge and ride straight across a meadow to cross another bridge. Turn left and ride up the beautiful Guller Creek Valley. Elk Ridge is at the head of the valley, just in sight.

7.9 Pass the remnants of an old cabin on the left. Jacque Ridge rises behind the old cabin.

10.4 Janets Cabin (10th Mountain Hut System) is below and on the left.

11.2 Summit of Searle Pass at 12,040 feet! Enjoy the view, and descend by the same route. If you would like to explore a little farther, the trail continues to Elk Ridge and Kokomo Pass, and Camp Hale and Tennessee Pass beyond that. See option, below.

22.4 Back at your car!

Option: Kokomo Pass is 3 miles beyond Searle Pass. The high point on Elk Ridge is about 2 miles. To continue to Camp Hale or Tennessee Pass involves a long shuttle: From Copper Mountain, drive south on Highway 91 over Fremont Pass. Just before Leadville, turn right on Highway 24. Drive over Tennessee Pass and continue 2.4 miles to the where the Colorado Trail crosses the Highway and park here on the left. To shorten the ride and end in Camp Hale, drive 1/2 mile past this parking area on Hwy. 24 to the unmarked Forest Road 726 and turn right. Follow this dirt road 3 miles and turn left on Forest Road 714. Drive 7/10ths of a mile to the CT trailhead on the right and leave a car here. Return to Copper Mountain and start the ride. The ride in the opposite direction from Camp Hale to Copper Mountain is also a good ride, but a more difficult climb. 🚲

Colorado Trail: Guller Creek

Colorado Trail: Searle Pass Summit

Colorado Trail: Searle Pass

Bald Mountain Road

SON OF MIDDLE CREEK • LOST LAKE
BUFFEHER CREEK TRAILS

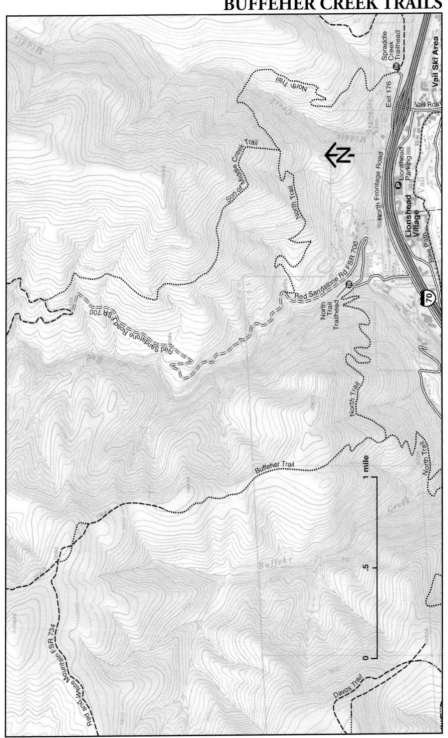

SON OF MIDDLE CREEK TRAIL
Ride Information

Description:

The Son of Middle Creek Trail is a smooth, pine needle covered trail perfect for mountain biking. This loop starts in Vail, climbing Red Sandstone Road and The Son of Middle Creek singletrack through mixed stands of pine and aspen. Finish off the loop with a fast descent on The Son of Middle Creek and The North Trails. This is a great autumn ride. The trails are non-motorized. Watch for vehicles on Red Sandstone Road.

Distance: 9 mile loop, 3.2 miles of dirt road, 4.4 miles of singletrack, 1.4 miles of pavement.

Time: 1 ½-2 hours.

Overall Difficulty: Intermediate

Technical Skill: Intermediate

Aerobic Effort: Moderately high

Elevation: Top: 9,600' Gain: 1,600'

Season: June 15 through early October. This area is closed May 1 through June 15 for Elk calving.

Usage: Moderate

Finding Route: Easy

Location: Start at the North Trail Trailhead on Red Sandstone Road in Vail. To get here, drive 9/10ths of a mile west on the North Frontage Road from Vail exit 176 to Red Sandstone Road. Turn right and continue 4/10ths of a mile up Red Sandstone Road to the parking area on the left. For alternate parking at the Spraddle Creek Trailhead, take Vail exit 176 and drive east on the North Frontage Road. Continue 2/10ths of a mile to the Spraddle Creek parking area. Ride to Red Sandstone Road to start the loop.

Maps: Latitude 40 Summit County Colorado Trails, or Sky Terrain Summit, Vail, and Holy Cross

Mileage Log:

0.0 Begin riding up Red Sandstone Road from the The North Trail Trailhead.

0.3 Ride straight ahead off the pavement as it switchbacks, onto the dirt continuation of Red Sandstone Road.

0.9 Pass the North Trail on the right. Continue up the road.

3.0 Turn right at the fork in the road, onto Lost Lake Road 786.

3.2 Turn right on the Son of Middle Creek singletrack, marked only with a pole. (If you arrive at a winter closure gate on Road 786, you have gone a little too far.) The trail climbs through an old clear cut, and enters the forest.

4.0 Top of the first climb.

4.8 Top out again. Begin a fast descent.

5.3 Arrive at a T-intersection with the North Trail. Turn left and descend. (Right here is 1.6 miles of smooth switchbacking descent back to Red Sandstone Road, where a left leads back to the trailhead.)

6.6 Cross a bridge and climb a short steep hill. More fast descent.

7.6 End of the trail at Spraddle Creek Trailhead. Turn right, passing the Vail exit 167 traffic circle, and ride west on the North Frontage Road and bike path.

8.7 Turn right onto Red Sandstone Road. ᗝᕐᐤ

BUFFEHER TRAIL

See map page 104-105 —————————— ### Ride Information

Description:

This excellent loop combines the steady climb of Red Sandstone Road with the smooth, fast descent of the non-motorized Buffeher and North Trails. The Buffeher Trail is a beautiful, hard-packed and fast singletrack through huge stands of aspen. The North Trail, a contouring trail made with mountain biking in mind, finishes off the loop, right in Vail. Expect and be courteous of other users on the loop. Don't miss this loop, it is one of the best!

Distance: 14.2 mile loop, 3/10ths of a mile paved road, 9 miles of dirt road, 5.2 miles of singletrack.

Time: 2-3 hours

Overall Difficulty: Advanced Intermediate

Technical Skill: Advanced intermediate with short sections of expert on the descent

Aerobic Effort: Moderately high

Elevation: Top: 10,200', Gain: 2,600'

Season: June 15 through early October. Closed May 1- June15 for elk calving.

Usage: Moderate

Finding Route: Easy

Location: Begin at the North Trail Trailhead on Red Sandstone Road in Vail. To get here, take Vail exit 176 and drive west on the North Frontage Road 9/10ths of a mile to Red Sandstone Road. Turn right and drive 4/10ths of a mile to the parking area on the left.

Maps: Latitude 40 Summit County Trails

Mileage Log:

0.0 Turn left out of the parking area and ride up the paved Red Sandstone Road.

0.3 Ride straight ahead off the pavement on a switchback, and continue on the now dirt Red Sandstone Road.

BUFFEHER TRAIL
Ride Information

0.9 Pass the North Trail to the right.

3.0 Turn left at the fork in the road, staying on Forest Road 700. Descend and cross a creek and climb again.

6.4 Ride around a switchback in an open meadow, and pass a campsite on the left. Ride around another switchback and climb into the dark timber.

7.0 Pass a campsite on the right.

7.1 Pass a private road on right.

7.2 Turn left on an old two track marked with big boulders and an old sign that the wording has worn off. This is a shortcut to Red and White Mountain Road. (If you miss the turn, continue about ½ mile to Red and White Mountain Road 734 and turn left. Continue to the signed Buffeher Trail.)

8.1 Turn left at a road fork in the camping area.

8.2 Merge left onto Red and White Mountain Road.

8.7 Turn left onto the signed Buffeher Trail, a doubletrack.

8.8 Take the less prominent spur to the right, which turns into a singletrack.

9.2 Cross the doubletrack in an open meadow and switchback down.

9.6 Merge right onto the road and ride downhill.

10.5 After the clearcut, enter the forest. The route turns to singletrack. Climb briefly and roll down this fast trail through the aspens. The trail has some steep and rutted sections, use caution.

12.0 Turn left on the North Trail and speed back on this fun contouring and switchbacking trail through the aspens and open hillsides.

14.2 Back to the parking lot. 🚲

LOST LAKE TO BUFFEHER TRAIL
Ride Information ———————————— *See map page 104-105*

Description:

This loop will take riders on a long climb through lots of aspen groves and past red rock walls to an awesome lunch spot at Lost Lake, with amazing views to the east of the Gore Mountains. The challenging, technical Lost Lake Trail leads back to the Red and White Mountain Road, and finally to the fast, steep and smooth Buffeher Creek Trail, that winds through more aspen groves. The ride finishes off with the North Trail, a great contouring trail that descends to Vail through aspens and oak hillside meadows. All in all, a classic ride. A wonderful fall ride.

Distance: 19.4 mile loop, .3 of pavement, 10 miles of dirt road, 9.1 miles of singletrack

Time: 3 ½ -4 ½ hours.

Overall Difficulty: Expert

Technical Skill: Expert

LOST LAKE TO BUFFEHER TRAIL
Ride Information

Aerobic Effort: High

Elevation: Top: 10,240', Gain: 3500'

Season: mid-June through October

Usage: Moderate to Heavy- expect to see other users on the Lost Lake Trail and be careful of heavy vehicle traffic on this popular road. Moderate on the Buffeher Trail.

Finding Route: Easy

Location: Start at the North Trail Trailhead on Red Sandstone Road in Vail. To get here, drive 9/10ths mile west on the North Frontage Road from Vail exit 176 to Red Sandstone Road. Continue 4/10ths of a mile to the parking area on the left.

Maps: Latitude 40 Summit County Trails or Sky Terrain Summit, Vail and Holy Cross.

Mileage Log

0.0   Turn left out of the parking area and ride up the paved Red Sandstone Road.

0.3   Ride straight ahead off pavement when pavement switchbacks right, and continue on the now dirt Red Sandstone Road.

0.9   Pass the North Trail off to the right.

3.0   Turn right on Lost Lake Road 786 at the fork.

3.2   Pass the beginning of the Son of Middle Creek Trail on the right.

3.7   Views of the Mount of the Holy Cross on the left.

4.4   Turn left on Road 786 at the fork in the road.

6.0   Continue straight ahead as you pass spur roads on the left and right. The road becomes much rockier and steeper after this point.

6.9   Stay right with Road 786.

7.2   Continue on Road 786 as it goes left and down.

7.3   Continue on Road 786 as it heads right and down, passing spur 786.1A to the left.

7.4   The Lost Lake Trail begins to the left of the sign. Ride down and cross Red Sandstone Creek. This section of the trail is technical and challenging.

8.1   Arrive at Lost Lake. Nice views of the Gore Mountains to the East. Turn right and east toward the Gore Mountains *before* the lake for the continuation of the trail, which is between the lake and the bog.

8.3   Arrive at a T-intersection. Turn left on this singletrack and climb. Negotiate more technical, some downhill and a stinger hill before two miles of fast downhill. Be careful to yield to other users on this heavily used trail.

11.7   End of the trail. Turn sharp left on Forest Service 700.

11.9   Take the first right onto Red and White Mountain Road 734. Climb on this rutted road.

12.6 Stay left on main road.

13.2 More views of the Gore Mountains.

14.0 Turn left onto the signed Buffeher Trail, a doubletrack at this point.

14.1 The road forks, take the less prominent spur to the right, which turns into a singletrack.

14.5 Cross the doubletrack in an open meadow and switchback down.

14.7 Merge right onto the road and ride downhill.

15.6 After a clearcut, enter the woods and ride onto the trail. Climb a short distance then zoom down this fast trail through the aspens. The trail has some steep and rutted sections.

17.1 Turn left on the North Trail and speed back on this fun contouring and switchbacking trail through the aspens and open hillsides.

19.3 Back to the parking lot. 🚲

Red and White Mountain Road

Buffeher Trail

THE NORTH TRAIL

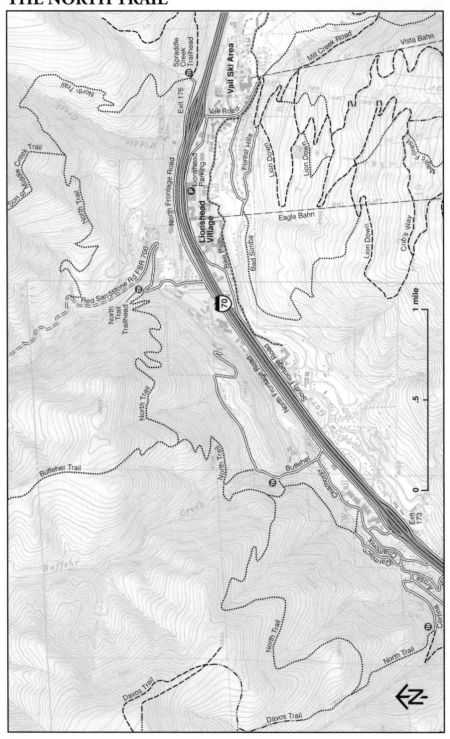

Description:

The North Trail is a classic singletrack along the north hillsides above Vail, built especially with mountain biking and hiking in mind. It has smooth, steady climbs, all rideable; and a variety of terrain from smooth and fast to technical and steep on the descents. It can be accessed from a variety of points, see location and options below. It is a good connector to the Davos Hill Climb from East Vail. The North Trail is easier from east to west, but for strong riders it is good west to east as well. Watch for other users on this popular trail. Lots of aspens line the trail, it makes a great autumn ride. The trail's only drawback is the sound of I70 can be heard from much of the trail. See Option 3 for a short beginner section of the North Trail.

Distance: 10.2 miles, 7.3 miles of singletrack, .4 miles of dirt road, 2.4 miles of pavement.

Time: 1 ½-2 ¼ hours

Overall Difficulty: Advanced intermediate with short expert sections

Technical Skill: Advanced intermediate to expert, tight switchbacks on the climb, and steep, rutted descents.

Aerobic Effort: Moderately high

Elevation: Top: 9,600' Gain: 2,100'

Season: This trail is closed from April 15-June 15 for elk calving. Open June 15-October

Usage: Moderate

Finding Route: Easy with a map and this guide. Junctions are signed but don't have names, only maps. I found these signs to be uninformative.

Location: Park at the North Trail Trailhead on Red Sandstone Road. To get here, take Vail exit 176 and drive west on the North Frontage Road 9/10ths of a mile to Red Sandstone Road. Turn right and drive 4/10ths of a mile to the parking lot on the left. An alternate starting point is The Spraddle Creek Trailhead. To get here, take Vail exit 176 and turn right onto the North Frontage Road. Drive east 2/10ths of a mile to the parking area. See option 1, below for ride directions from here.

Maps: Latitude 40 Summit County Trails or Sky Terrain Summit, Vail, and Holy Cross

Mileage Log:

0.0 Ride west out of the Red Sandstone Trailhead parking lot onto the singletrack. Begin switchbacking steadily up for about a mile, then contour and descend along the cliff top through beautiful aspens groves.

2.2 Ride straight ahead and descend past the Buffeher Trail, on the right. The descent becomes steep and technical. (The Buffeher Trail is quite steep at first, but can be ridden as an uphill by strong riders.)

2.7 Ride straight ahead, passing a closed spur to the left, and descend to Buffeher Creek.

2.8   Cross Buffeher Creek.

3.1   Turn right at the next intersection and climb steadily for ½ hour. (Turning left here and left again leads to the Buffeher Trailhead. See option 2 below.)

5.0   Top out at a great break spot with views of Holy Cross Mountain. Next, enjoy a smooth, fast descent through the aspens.

6.0   Turn left and descend as the Davos Trail merges in. This section of trail is steeper and more rutted, but hardpacked and fast.

6.6   Descend onto the Davos or Radio Tower Hill climb. Turn right and climb up the road.

7.0   Turn left through a gate and onto the signed North Trail.

7.7   End the North Trail, turn right and immediately left on the North Frontage Road. Ride carefully back to Red Sandstone road on the shoulder.

9.8   (approx. mileage) Turn left on Red Sandstone Road.

10.2   (approx. mileage) Back to the trailhead.

Option 1: To ride from the Spraddle Creek Trailhead: from Vail exit 167 turn right onto the North Frontage Road. Drive east 2/10ths of a mile to the parking area. Begin riding up the signed North Trail. Climb to the intersection with the Son of Middle Creek Trail at 2.3. Stay left here and descend gradual switchbacks to Red Sandstone Road at 3.9. Turn left and ride down the dirt then paved road .9 to the trailhead and continuation of the North Trail on the right. Continue with above directions from mile 0.0.

Option 2: Riding down to the Buffeher Trailhead: At mile 3.1, above, turn left. Again at 3.7 turn left. At 3.9 arrive at the Buffeher Trailhead. Turn right and ride .3 to the frontage road, where a left would take you back to Red Sandstone Road in 1.1 miles.

Option 3: To access the North Trail from The Buffeher Creek Trailhead, turn onto Buffeher Creek Road from the North Frontage Road and drive 1/4 mile to a parking area on the left. This first section is a good beginner introduction to singletrack: At the first intersection 0.2, ride straight ahead on this wonderful, smooth trail. At .07 continue straight onto Gamhearsh. Follow this to Ellefson Park and turn left on Arosa. Turn left on Chamonix Lane and follow this to Buffeher Drive, where another left would take you back to the trailhead. This is less than 2 miles long. ᚏᚒ

The North Trail Summit

The North Trail

NOTTINGHAM RIDGE & DAVOS TRAILS

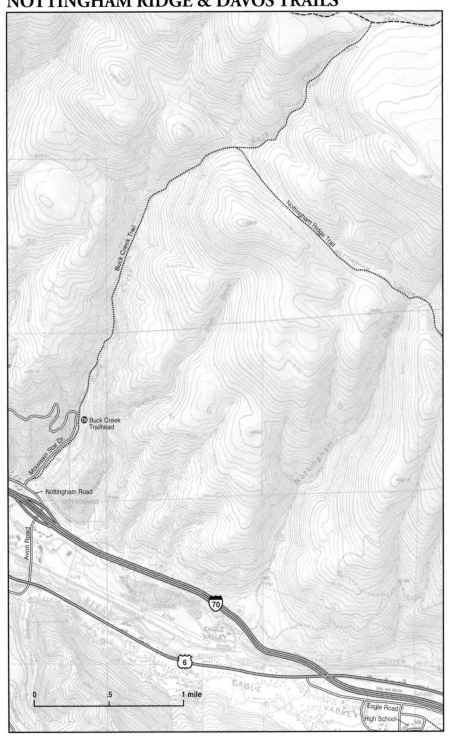

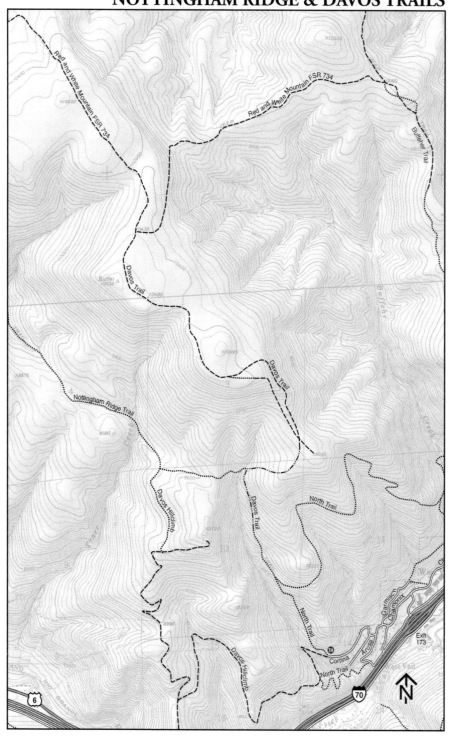

THE NOTTINGHAM RIDGE & DAVOS TRAILS
Ride Information

Description:

This is an awesome cross-country ride just outside of Vail. It climbs through dense forests and aspen groves, and into secluded stream-side mountain meadows. The Nottingham Trail is a non-system trail, so there are no signs and it is not maintained by the forest service, but it is easy to follow and quite enjoyable. This loop starts with the Davos or Radio Tower Hill Climb, a pleasant and mostly moderate climb starting in West Vail. After a beautiful trek on The Nottingham Ridge Trail, climb the challenging and steep Buck Creek Trail to the Red and White Mountain Road, and descend the steep, rutted, and difficult Davos Trail. A shorter shuttle option would be to descend the Buck Creek Trail and have a car parked at the trailhead in Avon, see options 1 and 3. The Nottingham Ridge Trail is great in reverse, accessed from the Red and White Mountain Road, see option 2. Riding up The Buck Creek Trail from Avon is a difficult and steep climb, but also offers access to The Nottingham Ridge Trail, see option 3. Wear orange in the fall during hunting season, and consider other rides during this time.

Distance: 15.9 mile loop; 9.2 miles of dirt road and four wheeler track, 6.7 miles of singletrack.

Time: 3 ½-5 hours

Overall Difficulty: Expert

Technical Skill: Expert

Aerobic Effort: High

Elevation: Top: 10,500' Gain: 3,100'

Season: late June -October

Usage: Light

Finding Route: Moderate. No signs on any turns, but the trails are fairly obvious.

Location: Begin this ride at the Davos Trailhead. To get here, take West Vail exit 173 and drive north onto Chamonix Road, right off the traffic circle. Follow the small Davos Trails signs. Drive 1/10th mile up Chamonix Road and turn left on Chamonix Lane. Drive 2/10ths mile and turn right on Arosa Lane, then immediately left staying on Arosa Lane. There is a small park here on the corner. Drive 2/10ths mile farther and turn right on Davos, then take an immediate right on Cortina. Follow this 1/4 mile to the trailhead, where there are a couple tight parking spots and a tight turn around area. Please do not block driveway or turn area. If you ride up, park at the City Market or Safeway parking areas just east of the west exit in Vail, on the North Frontage Road.

Maps: Sky Terrain Trail map for Summit, Vail and Holy Cross and Latitude 40 Summit County Trails

Mileage Log:

0.0   Begin riding up the dirt road that heads out of the parking lot.

THE NOTTINGHAM RIDGE & DAVOS TRAILS
Ride Information

0.1   Continue on the road, passing The Davos Trail on the right.

0.5   Continue up the road, passing The North Trail to the left.

1.3   Stay on the main road, passing a spur to the right.

2.2   Continue straight on the main road, passing a spur to the right.

2.5   Turn right at the road fork and ride around a gate, passing a spur to the left that leads to a radio tower.

3.3   Continue up and contour on the main road, passing a faint grassy spur that descends to the left. The road gets steeper and switchbacks up under the powerlines.

3.8   Ride through a gate and continue climbing.

4.2   Turn left on the unmarked Nottingham singletrack. The road continues straight to another radio tower.

4.8   Stay left when a spur trail merges in from the right. This sharp right spur leads to the Davos downhill trail, but is not a good uphill trail.

5.6   In the meadow, ride straight past a spur road on the left. There is an immediate fork in the singletrack, stay left.

8.8   Continue straight when a singletrack merges in on the right.

6.6   Stay right and cross Nottingham Creek, passing a less used trail on the left that descends the gulch. The trail becomes braided as it crosses another fork of the creek. After crossing, climb through beautiful meadows.

6.9   Pass a pond on the right.

7.0   Stay right at the next fork, and continue climbing on the singletrack in the meadow.

7.8   Top out and descend into the dark forest.

8.3   In the next meadow, turn right on the unmarked Buck Creek Trail. The climbing gets steep and challenging. (The Nottingham Ridge Trail continues straight ahead here, and the Buck Creek Trail descends the gulch. For a shorter loop, turn left onto the Buck Creek Trail. See option 1.)

9.3   Take the less steep trail to the left as a 4-wheeler track heads off right.

9.6   Turn right on Red and White Mountain Road. Pass two trails on the left in the next 2/10ths of a mile.

10.1   Continue right and into the forest passing a spur road that turns sharp left. (This is the Red and White Mountain Trail.) Climb and then descend past powerlines in an open meadow.

11.6   Pass a spur road on the right.

11.8   Turn right at the next road spur. There are two entrances to this road, and it is off a big corner of the road.

12.1   The doubletrack forks, stay left. Right leads to a campsite.

THE NOTTINGHAM RIDGE & DAVOS TRAILS
Ride Information

13.2 Just after rolling along the edge of the ridge, a singletrack forks to the right. Stay left on the road.

13.5 Ride around a corner and cross a doubletrack. Descend a four wheeler track. This is the Davos Trail. An old post and chain are here at the top.

13.8 Another four-wheeler track splits off left, continue down and right.

13.9 A singletrack cuts off to the right. This connects to mile 4.8 above and is a fun connector to the Nottingham Trail.

14.1 The four-wheeler track merges back in on the left. Continue descending.

14.5 The trail becomes less steep and narrows to a rutted singletrack.

15.1 Merge with The North Trail. Continue straight ahead and down this steep, hardpacked, and fast section.

15.8 The trail ends on the Davos Hill Climb Road. Turn left and descend to the trailhead.

15.9 Back to the trailhead.

Option 1: To descend The Buck Creek Trail, follow the directions above to mile 8.3. Have a shuttle set up at the Buck Creek Trailhead, see option 3.

8.3 Continue straight ahead less than 1/10th of a mile into the Buck Creek Gulch and turn left on the Buck Creek Trail. As the trail drops in next to the red rocks it becomes more distinct. This is a beautiful descent, at first narrow, then wider and gradual through the aspens.

10.2 Cross the creek to the left and walk your bike through a huge culvert next to the creek.

10.4 The trail gets very rocky and bushy. Cross the creek three times under the bridge.

10.5 Turn right and walk up to the parking area.

Option 2: To ride The Nottingham Ridge Trail as a descent, follow the directions to the Buffeher Trail, page 107, until mile 8.7.

8.7 Continue on Red and White Mountain Road, passing the Buffeher Trail to the left.

10.9 Pass a spur road to left.

11.1 Pass the Davos Trail (doubletrack) to the left.

11.3 Pass a spur road on the left.

12.8 Pass a spur road on the right, then pass 2 singletracks on the right.

13.3 Turn left on the unsigned Buck Creek. It is in a gulch near an old corral.

14.6 Turn left on the Nottingham Ridge Trail.

18.7 Turn right on the Davos Hill Climb Road.

22.4 Turn right on the signed North Trail.

23.1 Turn right, then left onto the North Frontage Road and follow this back to West Vail. Turn left on Chamonix Road and return to your car.

24.6 (approx. mileage.) Back to your car.

Option 3: To get to the Buck Creek Trailhead: Take the Avon exit 167 off I70 (west of Vail) and drive onto Nottingham Road heading west. Turn right on Mountain Star Drive in 2/10ths of a mile. Follow this ½ mile to the trailhead and parking on the left. The trail starts next to the creek below the parking area. 🚲

Nottingham Ridge Trail

Nottingham Ridge Trail

MEADOW MOUNTAIN & WHISKEY CREEK TRAILS

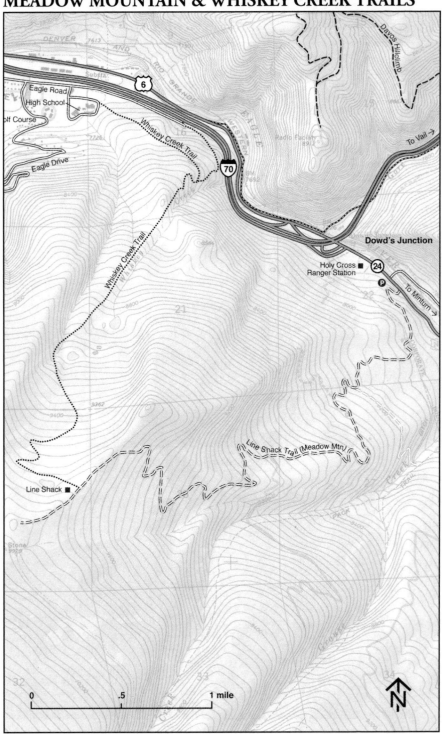

MEADOW MOUNTAIN & WHISKEY CREEK TRAILS
Ride Information

Description:

This is a wonderful, non-motorized loop of medium length. It starts with a moderately steep old two-track climb through beautiful grassy meadows and aspen groves on Meadow Mountain. At the top of the climb, near an historic cabin (the line shack,) riders are rewarded with views of the Gore Mountains, the Mosquito and Ten Mile Ranges, and beautiful wildflowers in July. The entire way down The Whiskey Creek Trail is twisty, turning singletrack through meadows and aspen groves, and fast, smooth sections that will get you giggling. The ride is located 4/10ths of a mile south of Dowd's Junction, on Highway 24. Dowd's Junction is about 3 miles west of Vail on I70. Part of the Whiskey Creek Trail is on State Land and is pending usage changes. Check with the Forest Service office at the start of the trail to find out if it is open to bikes. Use caution on the busy highway section that connects this loop.

Distance: 13.3 mile loop, 5 miles primitive dirt road, 3 miles pavement, 5.3 miles of singletrack.

Time: 2-3 hours

Overall Difficulty: Advanced intermediate

Technical Skill: Advanced intermediate

Aerobic Effort: Moderately high. The climb is continuous, and steep in sections.

Elevation: Top: 9,750' Gain: 2,250'

Season: July through early October. The Whiskey Creek Trail is closed through July 1 for elk calving. The Meadow Mountain Trail opens June 15, and is a nice out and back.

Usage: Moderate

Finding Route: Easy

Location: Start at the Holy Cross Forest Service Ranger District. This is located on Highway 24 on the way to Minturn from Dowd's Junction, about 3 miles west of Vail. The trail begins at the south end of the dirt parking lot next to the forest service office.

Maps: Latitude 40 Summit County Colorado Trails or Sky Terrain Summit, Vail and Holy Cross.

Mileage Log:

0.0   Start riding up the Meadow Mountain dirt road behind the forest service house and parking lot. This trail is closed to motorized vehicles. There is a trailhead sign and sign-in sheet here.

1.1   Pass a spur on the left to Grouse Creek. This leads to The Holy Cross Wilderness, no bikes allowed.

MEADOW MOUNTAIN & WHISKEY CREEK TRAILS
Ride Information

2.7   Stay right at the road fork. Ride through one of the many beautiful aspen groves on this ride.

5.0   Top out at an old cabin. Ride to the right and around the front of the cabin, then left and behind the cabin, where the trail descends to the northwest. Watch out for tight switchbacks and roots on this otherwise fast descent.

8.6   Turn left off the steep section of doubletrack, and contour then descend on singletrack.

9.3   Turn right when the trail forks just before the golf course.

9.4   Trail ends on a road behind the school. Turn left and ride out of the school lot.

9.5   Turn right, then left on Eagle Drive.

10.4   Eagle Drive intersects Highway 6. Turn right and ride along the shoulder, riding under I70.

11.8   Ride onto the bike path that begins on the left side of the road.

12.9   Stay right and carefully cross Highway 24 when the bike path crosses the river to the left. I70 is just ahead and above you. Ride under I70 and continue on the shoulder of the Highway 24.

13.3   Reach the forest service parking lot. ⚂

Meadow Mountain Trail

Whiskey Creek Trail

Whiskey Creek Trail

THE VILLAGE-TO-VILLAGE & PAULIE'S PLUNGE TRAILS

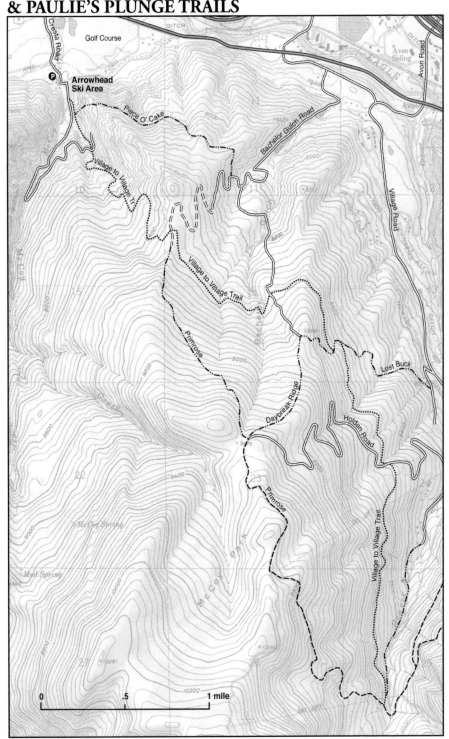

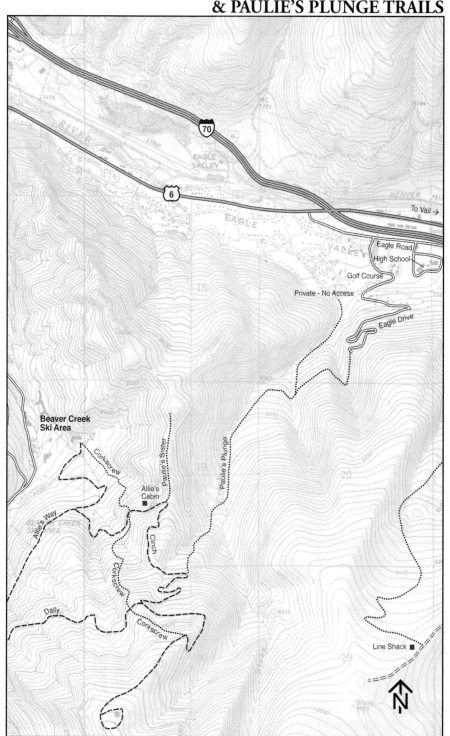

THE VILLAGE-TO-VILLAGE & PAULIE'S PLUNGE TRAILS
Ride Information

Description:

This trail begins at the Arrowhead Ski Area in Avon, climbing to a high traverse above the Eagle River Valley, and connects to the Beaver Creek Ski Area. The climb from Arrowhead is moderately steep, but the traversing section of the Village-to-Village Trail is wide, mostly flat, and easy. The loop described here finishes off with Paulie's Plunge, which is at first technical and then fast and smooth. This is the best route off the Beaver Creek Ski Area, but there are several alternate trails to explore. See Beaver Creek Summer Trail Map for details and locations.

Distance: 20.4 mile loop, 5 miles of singletrack, 6 miles of narrow non-motorized doubletrack, 2.8 miles of dirt road, and 7.2 miles of pavement.

Time: 3-4 ½ hours

Overall Difficulty: Expert. The Village to Village Trail is intermediate, Paulies Plunge and Corkscrew are expert.

Technical Skill: Expert

Aerobic Effort: Moderately High

Elevation: Top: 9,500' Gain: 2,400'

Season: July 1 through early October. Paulie's Plunge is closed from May 1 to June 30th for Elk calving.

Usage: Moderate, watch for other users on the trails and roads.

Finding Route: Moderate. Most turns are marked, but the trail traverses ski runs and private land, much of which is under construction, which makes certain areas confusing.

Location: Begin at the tennis parking lot at the base of Arrowhead Ski Area. To get here, drive 1.7 miles east of Edwards Road, in Edwards, or 2 miles west of Beaver Creek on Highway 6. Drive into Arrowhead and past the gate person, continue ¼ mile and turn left on Cresta Road. Turn right in 1/10th of a mile into the parking area.

Maps: Latitude 40 Summit County Trails, Sky Terrain Summit, Vail and Holy Cross, and the Beaver Creek summer trails map.

Mileage Log:

0.0 Turn right out of the parking lot and begin riding up the paved Cresta Road.

0.1 Ride through a gate.

0.4 Turn left onto a dirt road under the Arrow Bahn Express lift and below the condos. Swing right and climb gradually.

0.5 Turn left onto the signed Village-to-Village Trail under the quad lift.

0.9 Continue on the Village-to-Village Trail, passing a spur road to the right.

THE VILLAGE-TO-VILLAGE
& PAULIE'S PLUNGE TRAILS
Ride Information

1.0   Turn right and climb steeply on the signed Village-to-Village Trail.

1.7   Ride under a large bridge and paved road in an area of homes. Turn left and climb a dirt road.

2.1   Turn right on the Village-to-Village singletrack marked with a hiker sign. The trail is flat and starts off a switchback, then climbs by gradual switchbacks, then contours.

3.3   Ride onto a subdivision road, across from a building. Turn left and descend this road, passing a trail to the left, and ride under a large bridge. Climb up the dirt road, passing private homes.

3.5   The trail is braided in this area. Switchback up below the steep hill and turn left on the now obvious trail.

4.1   Ride straight ahead, passing Andersons Trail on the left.

4.3   Cross a wooden bridge over a swampy area.

4.4   Stay left and climb over a bridge. Continue on doubletrack.

4.5   Stay left and descend, passing the Daybreak Ridge Trail, a doubletrack that climbs to the right.

4.6   After riding down two switchbacks on the doubletrack, turn hard right onto a narrower section of trail. This is a fun, smooth, rolling section.

5.6   Cross Holden Road. Continue straight on the Village-to-Village Trail.

6.0   Merge onto a road, turn left and descend some switchbacks, then turn right. Continue traversing.

7.3   Cross a bridge.

7.4   Arrive at a T intersection, turn right and climb toward Beaver Lake, leaving the Village-to-Village Trail. Left descends to Beaver Creek Village in 1.7 miles.

7.5   Turn left onto a major road, Dally's. Ride downhill and below the Grouse Creek Lift.

7.7   Stay right and climb, passing the Birds of Prey lift on the left.

8.6   Pass the Overlook Trail on the left, and the Dally hiking trail on the right.

9.0   Turn left onto the signed, steep and rooted Corkscrew Trail. (Or see option 1, below to bypass this trail.)

9.8   Stay right.

9.9   Turn right when you intersect Cinch Road, and ride uphill. (Corkscrew continues to the bottom of the Beaver Creek Ski Area if you want to try a different route down.)

10.0   Pass Allie's Cabin Restaurant on the left.

10.3   Pass Paulie's Sister Trail on the left of a switchback. This trail is hidden in the bushes, and difficult to follow.

THE VILLAGE-TO-VILLAGE & PAULIE'S PLUNGE TRAILS
Ride Information

10.7 Look for the red firebox bench and the user sign to find the Paulies Plunge Trail. This area is closed until June 30 for Elk Calving. The trail starts out with a bang.

11.4 Cross a bridge and ride through a rocky section.

11.8 The trail turns smooth and fast.

12.5 At the trail intersection, stay right and cross the draw riding up onto the flume bank. Left descends to the Beaver Creek Golf Course.

13.2 End on a paved road. Turn left and descend Eagle Drive.

13.6 Sharp left at the switchback.

14.5 Turn left, staying on Eagle Drive.

14.9 Turn left on Highway 6, and ride back to the Avon roundabout. Cross the roundabout carefully, and continue on Highway 6; or turn right on Avon Road and cross the Eagle River to the bike path. Follow this back to Arrowhead.

20.0 Back to Arrowhead, turn left and ride 4/10ths back to your vehicle.

20.4 End at your car.

Option 1: To bypass the Corkscrew Trail at 9.5, continue on Dally Road until you intersect Cinch Road. Turn left and ride down to the red firebox that marks the beginning of the trail.

Option 2: Paulie's Plunge is also accessible by riding up through Beaver Creek, crossing the Village-to-Village Trail (mile 7.4, above,) and following the directions from here. 🚴

The Grand Traverse Trail, Vail Mountain

Village to Village Trail

Bowmans Shortcut Trail

TWO ELK CREEK TRAIL

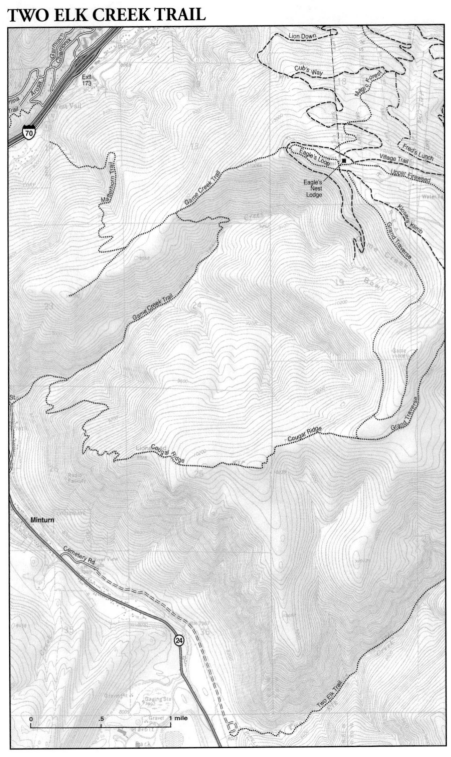

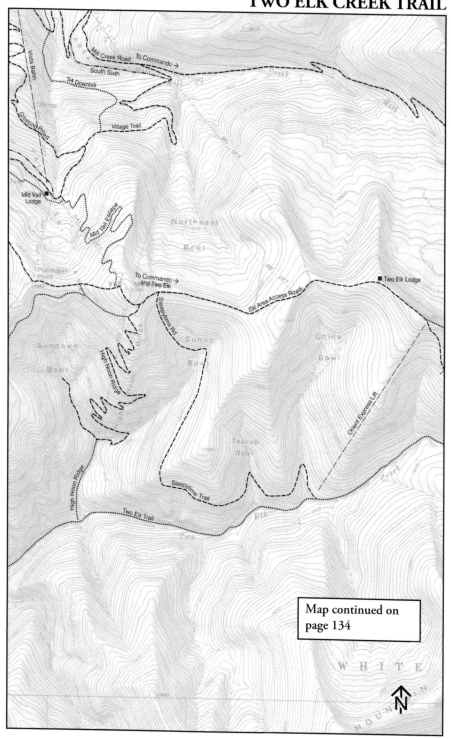

Map continued on page 134

BOWMANS SHORTCUT TRAIL

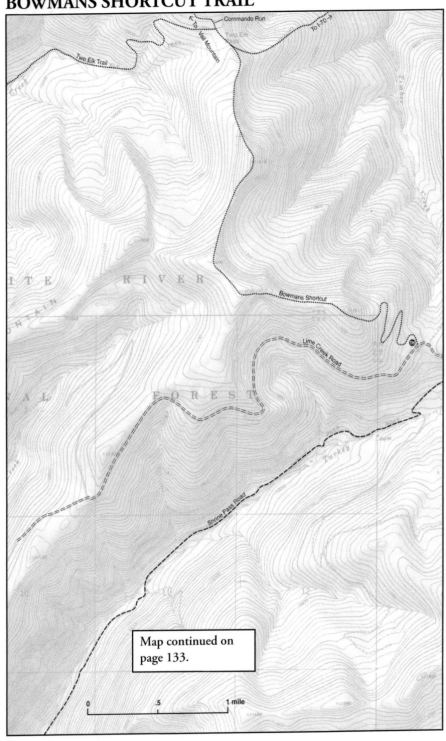

Commando Run

To Vail Mountain

Two Elk Trail

Two Elk Trail

To I-70

Bowmans Shortcut

Lime Creek Road

Turkey

Shrine Pass Road

FOREST

RIVER

Map continued on page 133.

0   .5   1 mile

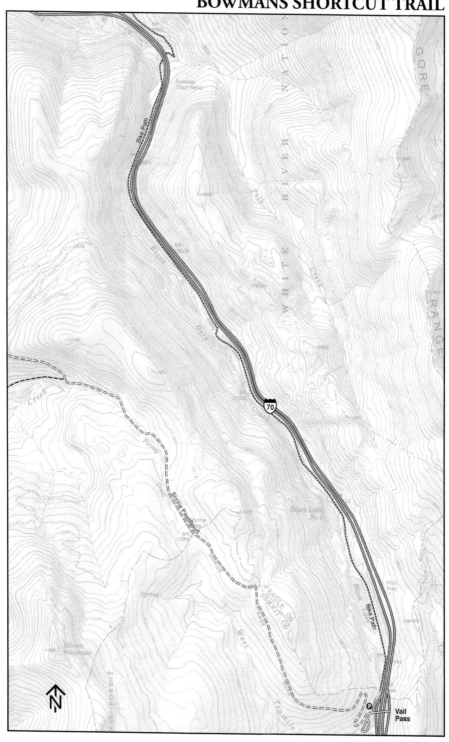

TWO ELK CREEK & BOWMANS SHORTCUT TRAILS
Ride Information

Description:

Don't miss this spectacular ride! It travels through a variety of terrain, from dense pine forests to high alpine meadows, through huge aspen groves and along the beautiful Two Elk Creek. It is quite pristine. Two Elk is described here using a shuttle up Vail Pass. The ride starts with a roll along scenic Shrine Pass Road and then climbs the challenging Bowman's Shortcut Trail. From a spectacular viewpoint descend to the Two Elk Trail, a challenging and technical ride down to Minturn. Two Elk Creek can also be accessed from Vail Mountain, skipping the Bowman's Shortcut Trail, see option 1. Two Elk Creek can be ridden as a very large loop, connected by riding the paved recreation path from Dowd's Junction to the top of Vail Pass, adding 21 miles.

Distance: 19.6 miles with a shuttle: 6.5 miles of dirt road, 1 mile of paved road, 12.1 miles of singletrack. Add 5 ½ miles if you ride up Vail Mountain.

Time: 3 ½ -4 ½ hours with a shuttle. Add 1-3 hours to connect as a loop.

Overall Difficulty: Expert

Technical Skill: Expert

Aerobic Effort: Moderately high as a shuttle. High if ridden as a loop with Vail Mountain or the bike path, moderate with Vail Mountain lift access.

Elevation: Top: 11,700' Gain: 2,250'. Add 2,800' if you ride up the bike path, or 1,000' if you ride up the ski area.

Season: Late June through October

Usage: Light to Moderate. Expect traffic on Shrine Pass Road and the bike path.

Finding Route: Easy from Bowmans, moderate from Vail Mountain

Location: To do a shuttle, leave a vehicle in Minturn, 1.7 miles south of I70 from Dowd's Junction, on Highway 24. Drive a second car to the top of Vail Pass via I70. Just past the huge CDOT sand barn and the summit of Vail Pass is the exit to Shrine Pass Road. Turn right and park parallel to the highway.

Maps: Latitude 40 Summit County Trails

Mileage Log:

0.0 Turn right out of the parking lot and ride straight onto the Shrine Pass dirt road, and begin climbing.

1.6 Stay on the main road, passing a spur to the right.

2.3 Stay on the main road, passing a trailhead for Wilder Creek on the left.

3.9 Pass a viewpoint trail and gauging station on the left, then descend briefly to the signed Lime Creek Road. Turn right.

4.4 Turn left at the next road junction on Forest Road 712.

4.5 Turn right on the signed Bowmans Shortcut singletrack. Climb for 1 ½ miles, with some welcome breaks.

7.1 Top out in a high alpine meadow with great views of the Gore Mountains, Holy Cross, and the Ten Mile Range. Ride northwest on the singletrack, crossing a faint doubletrack.

7.5 Another awesome view of the Gore Mountains! From here descend steeply.

9.2 Arrive at Two Elk Pass. Ride straight ahead. (Right leads down to I70, left is the old trail and now dead-ends.)

9.4 The Commando Trail comes in on the right. Stay left and ride under the ski area boundary rope, and descend on rutted switchbacks into the big Two Elk Creek valley.

11.8 Ride above the Orient Express lift, then cross a faint grassy doubletrack, the Sleepytime Trail.

12.0 Descend onto a major access road and turn right. Turn immediately left onto the trail and descend along the creek on its' steep bank.

14.0 Cross a side creek and the High Noon Ridge Trail from Vail Mountain. Continue down the creek.

16.3 Cross to the left bank of Two Elk Creek on a good bridge. The trail opens up and is smooth and fast.

17.0 End of the trail near Highway 24. Stay right and parallel the highway.

17.1 Cross Two Elk Creek on a bridge and stay on the lower trail, then follow the dirt road back toward Minturn.

18.9 Merge left onto the paved Cemetery Road. Cross a bridge and turn right on Highway 24. The road is narrow here, without much shoulder.

19.6 End at the corner bridge in Minturn.

OPTION 1: To access the Two Elk Trail from Vail Mountain: Ride up Mill Creek Road to the very top to intersect the Two Elk Trail, see your Latitude 40 map for details. Or follow the directions for Vail Mountain, Grand Traverse to Mid-Vail Escape to mile 11.3, then:

11.3 Intersect another service road. Nice views of the Gore Mountains and a ski sign for "The Slot." Turn right and descend this road, heading to the east.

11.4 Stay left and climb, passing the Sleepytime Road to the right.

12.1 Stay right and continue climbing, passing a spur road to the left.

12.5 Reach a saddle and a road junction. Turn left toward the big Two Elk Lodge.

12.6 Turn right and ride in front of the Two Elk Lodge.

12.7 Ride onto a road to the right of the Poma Lift and climb. Merge with another road at the top and head right along the ridge.

13.3 Just past the Orient Express lift look for a singletrack on your left. This is an unmarked shortcut to the Commando Run. Follow this along below a bluff, and then follow the trail to hike your bike up onto the small bluff. Continue right.

13.8 Turn right at a fork in the singletrack, and descend a little.

14.0 Arrive at the top of a poma lift. Ride left around the lift shack and straight ahead onto the grassy doubletrack. Look for a ski sign, "Silk Road." It soon narrows to singletrack and switchbacks down. (Don't go right down the steep lift line!)

15.4 Intersect the Two Elk Trail, at mile 9.4 in the Two Elk Creek, Bowmans Shortcut description above.

When you reach Minturn, continue through town and another 1.7 miles. Ride under I70, turn right on the bike path and cross the Eagle River. Follow this back along Gore Creek to the South Frontage Road, and follow this back to the Lionshead Parking. Lionshead Parking is located 6/10th's of a mile west of Vail Exit 176, and is free parking for all summer Vail activities. 🚲

Bowmans Shortcut Trail

Bowmans Shortcut Trail

Two Elk Creek Trail

VAIL MOUNTAIN SKI AREA

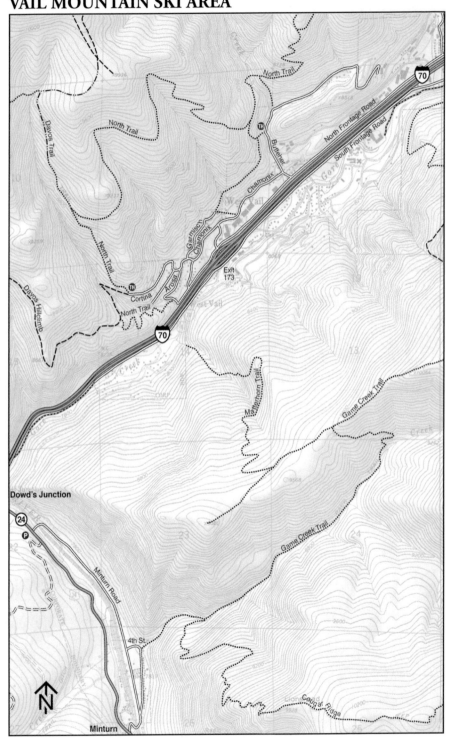

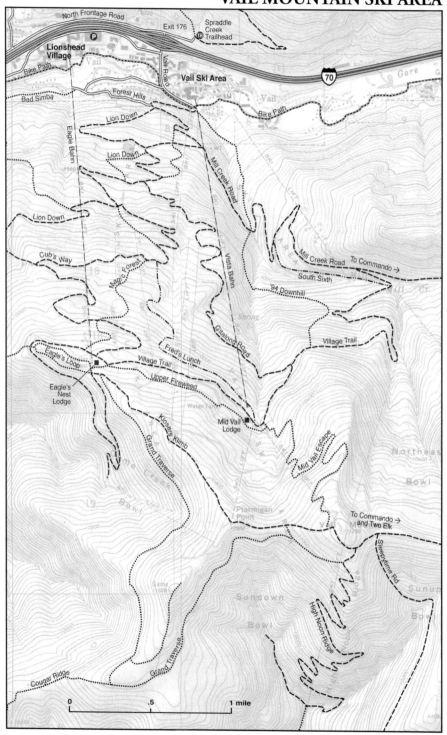

VAIL MOUNTAIN
GRAND TRAVERSE TO MID-VAIL ESCAPE
Ride Information

Description:

This loop combines a gradual climb on The Village Trail and Upper Fireweed to Eagle's Nest on Vail Mountain, a beautiful high traverse of the back bowls on The Grand Traverse, and a fun intermediate descent back down to the Lionshead Base area on Mid-Vail Escape. Fred's Lunch, and Lions Down. Mid-Vail escape is mostly singletrack. Fred's Lunch and most of the lower trails on Vail Mountain are old doubletrack, but still fun descents. The Lionsdown and Gitalong Roads are alternate ways to the top, and the Vail Ski Area offers lift tickets throughout the summer for access to Eagle's Nest, which brings you right to the start of the Grand Traverse and several other fun trails. Tickets and summer trail maps are available at the Lionshead ticket office. This office is located down the stairs from the Lionshead parking structure and through the shopping area and right, near the base of the Lionshead gondola.

Distance: 17.4 mile loop, 6.5 miles of singletrack, .5 miles of paved road, 10.4 miles of dirt road.

Time: 3-4 hours

Overall Difficulty: Advanced Intermediate

Technical Skill: Intermediate

Aerobic Effort: Moderate

Elevation: Top: 11,250' Gain: 3,250'

Season: Late June through early October

Usage: Moderate, light when summer season is over

Finding Route: Moderate. There are lots of turns; the ski area is well marked during the summer season.

Maps: Latitude 40 Summit County Trails and the Vail Mountain summer trails map

Location: Park at the Lionshead parking structure. To get here drive west on the South Frontage Road .6 miles from Vail exit 176, and turn left just before the information center. From here, ride back on the frontage road to the exit and turn right on Vail Road. Start your mileage here.

Mileage Log:

0.0   Turn right on Vail Road. Stay on the shoulder.

0.2   Stay right on Vail Road.

0.4   Ride under the Vista Bahn Quad lift. The road turns to dirt. Begin climbing.

0.7   Turn left on Mill Creek Road at its junction with Forest Road.

1.1   Stay left toward Mid-Vail, passing the bottom of Gitalong Road.

2.3   Pass the bottom of the South 6th Trail.

3.4 Stay right at a road intersection and descend through a gate. The left fork is the continuation of Mill Creek Road. Pass the bottom of Chair 10.

3.6 The South 6th doubletrack descends on the right. Stay left and continue climbing.

4.0 On a switchback, pass the 94 Downhill Trail.

4.6 Stay right on The Village Trail, passing the Northwoods Express Lift and spur road on the left.

5.4 Ride straight ahead on the Village Trail, as Gitalong Road descends on the right.

5.6 The start of the 94 Downhill is the right.

5.8 Arrive at Mid-Vail. Either continue following the Village Trail road straight past the Mid-Vail Lodge and on to Eagle's Nest, or try a more fun route by turning left just before the Mid-Vail Lodge. Climb up just above the lodge and turn left, riding toward a three-way junction.

5.9 At the junction, turn right on Upper fireweed.

6.0 Turn right on Upper Fireweed and contour.

6.2 Merge onto a road.

6.4 Stay left with the singletrack as the road descends.

6.7 Cross a road, continue straight on singletrack.

7.0 Turn left on The Village Trail road. Turn left just before the gondola building, then turn right and ride behind the building to the junction of several roads and trails. This is Eagles Nest.

7.2 Just left of the "Game Trail" ski sign and a descending road is Kloser's Klimb. Ride up this rocky doubletrack briefly and turn right, and turn right again as the Grand Traverse singletrack begins. This trail starts out flat and smooth.

7.7 Cross a faint doubletrack.

8.8 Cross under the ski area boundary ropes and start climbing gradually.

9.1 Ride straight through an intersection. A sharp left takes you to Wildwood.

9.3 Stay left on the Grand Traverse as the unmarked Cougar Ridge Trail turns off to the right.

9.4 Ride back under the boundary ropes. Continue traversing and climbing gradually.

10.7 Climb more steeply, in the forest now.

10.8 Stay right at a trail intersection. Left is a shortcut to Kloser's Klimb.

11.1 Turn left and up on the service road.

11.3 Intersect another service road. Nice views of the Gore Mountains. At this junction is a ski sign for "The Slot." Turn left and ride uphill.

VAIL MOUNTAIN
GRAND TRAVERSE TO MID-VAIL ESCAPE
Ride Information

11.4 Continue straight ahead, passing the continuation of the Klosers doubletrack and buildings on the right. Ride over the top of the hill and start downhill on the main road. Pass another spur road to the right.

11.6 Turn right onto the Mid-Vail Escape singletrack. Switchback down.

13.7 Turn right at the three-way junction above the Mid-Vail Lodge. Descend to the lodge and turn right again. Descend briefly to the Village Trail road, and turn left.

13.8 Right below the Mid-Vail Lodge, turn right on Fred's Lunch doubletrack.

14.4 Stay left.

14.6 Stay left as the trail narrows.

14.9 Back on a doubletrack. Cross a singletrack. Ride down a few switchbacks.

15.3 Pass the top of a lift. As the road switchbacks to the right, ride straight ahead onto the singletrack and toward Lionshead.

15.6 Turn right and descend.

15.7 Turn right onto a road, and immediately turn left onto the Lionsdown singletrack.

16.0 Stay right.

16.2 Continue straight, crossing Berry Picker.

16.3 Cross Berry Picker again.

16.4 Continue straight across the road to the singletrack.

16.5 Back onto doubletrack, continue downhill.

16.6 Stay left on singletrack.

16.9 Stay left on the road.

17.0 Turn right onto a road at the T-intersection. Watch for downhillers coming down.

17.2 Turn left at the intersection with Mill Creek Road and Forest Road. Continue straight ahead, passing Beaver Dam Road, then turning right above the gondola and cross the Lionshead Bridge to the base area.

17.7 Back to the base area. 🚲

Description:

This loop combines a moderate climb up the Lions Down Trail and a steep descent of The Game Creek Trail into Minturn. A short stint on Highway 24 and the paved bike path completes the loop. Lions Down is a combination of singletrack and dirt road, with many junctions. It is well marked during the summer season, which makes it easier to follow. The entire ride boasts huge stands of aspens, an absolute joy in the fall. The descent on The Game Creek Trail follows a sunny ridge, then turns left and becomes quite steep. The route then mellows and follows Game Creek back to Minturn. The Vail Village Trail and Gitalong Road are optional routes up the mountain. Lift tickets are available throughout the summer season for access to the top of Eagle's Nest if you prefer skipping the ride up the mountain. Tickets and summer trail maps are available at the Lionshead ticket office. This office is located down the stairs from the parking structure and through the shopping area and right, near the base of the Lionhead Gondola.

Distance: 16.3 miles, 4.3 miles of singletrack, 6 miles of dirt road, and 6 miles of pavement.

Time: 2 ½ -3 ½ hours

Overall Difficulty: Expert

Technical Skill: Expert

Aerobic Effort: Moderately high

Elevation: Top 10,400' Gain: 2,675'

Season: July through early October. Closed for elk calving before July.

Usage: light

Finding Route: Moderate to Difficult

Location: Park at the Lionshead free parking structure. To get here drive west on the South Frontage Road .6 miles from Vail exit 176, and turn left just before the information center. Carry your bike down the stairs and right toward the base of the gondola. Start here. (If the Lionshead Bridge is still closed for construction, ride left on the paved bike path to Vail Road and right to to the junction of Forest Road and Mill Creek Road. Turn right here (see mile 0.8 below.)

Maps: Latitude 40 Summit County Trails and Vail Mountain summer trails map.

Mileage Log:

0.0 Begin at the base of the Lionshead Gondola. Ride straight over the Lionshead Bridge and turn left, climbing. Ride under the Gondola.

0.3 Stay right, passing Beaver Dam road.

0.5 Stay high on Forest Road. This paved road soon turns to dirt.

0.8 Arrive at an intersection on a switchback in the Mill Creek Road (Vail Village Loop.) There is a small ski area building and an emergency phone to the left. Turn right on the Lions Down doubletrack (not Mill Creek Road.)

0.9   Turn left at fork in road. Right and up is the Mane Lane doubletrack.

1.1   Continue on the road, passing a flat singletrack to the left.

1.3   Turn right on a singletrack that bypasses a short steep hill on the road.

1.4   The road turns to singletrack. Continue climbing.

1.5   Cross a road and continue climbing on singletrack.

1.6   Cross the Berry Picker hiking trail.

1.7   Cross Berry Picker again, continue straight.

1.9   Continue straight, passing a hiking spur that heads up and right.

2.1   Turn right at the fork in the road and climb. Gitalong Road heads left.

2.8   Stay right on the main road, passing a spur road. Continue climbing on long switchbacks through the aspens.

4.2   Stay right, passing Cubs Way Road and the Born Free lift to the left.

4.9   Stay right with the main road around a switchback. Minnies ski sign to left.

6.1   Arrive at the top of the gondola. Ride to the right of the building, and then left and up between the gondola building and the Pride Express lift.

6.3   Turn right onto the Eagles Loop singletrack, just above the Pride Express.

6.4   Stay left at the trail fork.

6.5   Turn right on the edge of the ridge, leaving the Eagle's Loop, and descend.

6.6   Drop steeply onto a dirt road, cross it, and descend the unmarked singletrack along the ridge through the aspens. The trail is at first steep, then more gradual.

7.5   Turn left at fork and head steeply down. This appears to be the less used trail, but don't miss this turn! The right fork is a very steep user created trail with several spurs. If you miss this turn and end up on a paved cul-de-sac above I70, work your way down and right and back to the Lionshead base.

9.5   (approx mileage) Join the Cougar Ridge Trail.

10.0   (approx mileage) End of the trail in a Minturn neighborhood. Descend to 4th Street.

10.2   (approx mileage) Turn right on 4th Street.

10.5   (approx. mileage) Turn right on Minturn Road and follow this north. Cross the Eagle River.

11.2   (approx. mileage) Turn right on Highway 24.

11.8   (approx mileage) Ride under I70 and turn right onto the bike path, crossing the Eagle River. Continue on the bike path along Gore Creek back to West Vail. At a park, begin riding on the South Frontage Road. Stay on the shoulder.

16.3   (approx. mileage) Back to the Lionshead parking. 🚲

Description:

This loop combines the meandering Vail Village Trail up Vail Mountain with the awesome descent of The Cougar Ridge Trail into Minturn. A short stint on Highway 24 and the paved bike path completes the loop. Riders are treated with views of The Holy Cross Mountain and fast descents through large stands of aspen. The Vail Village Trail loops away from a lot of the summer activity, and travels through big groves of aspens, making it a nice autumn ride. Lions Down and Gitalong Road are optional routes up the mountain. Lift tickets are available throughout the summer season for access to the top of Eagle's Nest if you prefer skipping the ride up the mountain. Tickets and summer trail maps are available at the Lionshead ticket office. This office is located down the stairs from the Lionshead parking structure and through the shopping area and right, near the base of the gondola.

Distance: 21 mile loop, 6 miles of dirt road, 8 miles of singletrack, 6 miles of pavement.

Time: 3-4 hours

Overall Difficulty: Expert

Technical Skill: Expert

Aerobic Effort: Moderate

Elevation: Top: 10,750' Gain: 3,225'

Season: July through early October. Closed for elk calving before July.

Usage: Low to moderate

Finding Route: Easy

Location: Park at the Lionshead Free parking. To get here drive west on the South Frontage Road .6 miles from Vail exit 176, and turn left just before the information center. From here, ride back on the frontage road to the roundabout and turn right on Vail Road. Start your mileage here.

Maps: Latitude 40 Summit County Trails and the Vail Mountain bike trails map

Mileage Log:

0.0 Turn right on Vail Road. Stay on the shoulder.

0.2 Stay right on Vail Road.

0.3 Climb under the Vista Bahn Quad lift. The road turns to dirt.

0.7 Turn left on Mill Creek Road at the junction with Forest Road.

1.1 Stay left toward Mid-Vail, passing the bottom of Gitalong Road.

2.3 Pass the bottom of the South 6th Trail.

3.4 Stay right at a major fork in the road, and descend through a closed gate. (Left is the continuation of Mill Creek Road.)

3.5 Pass the bottom of Chair 10 on a switchback.

3.6 The South 6th doubletrack descends on the right. Stay left and continue up the Village Trail.

VAIL MOUNTAIN
THE COUGAR RIDGE TRAIL
Ride Information

4.0	Pass the 94 Downhill Trail on a switchback.
4.6	Stay right on the Village Trail, passing the Northwoods Express Lift and spur road on the left.
5.4	Stay left on the Village Trail, as Gitalong Road descends to the right.
5.6	The 94 Downhill starts on the right.
5.8	Arrive at Mid-Vail. Either continue following the Village Trail straight past the Mid-Vail Lodge and on to Eagle's Nest, or try a singletrack route, described here. Turn left just before The Mid-Vail Lodge on doubletrack. Climb up behind the building and turn left. Follow this briefly.
5.9	Turn right at a three-way junction.
6.0	Turn right on Upper Fireweed and contour.
6.2	Merge onto a road.
6.4	Stay left with the singletrack as the road descends.
6.7	Cross a road, continue straight on singletrack.
7.0	Turn left on The Village Trail road. Turn left again just before the gondola building, then turn right and ride behind the building to the junction of several roads and trails. This is Eagles Nest.
7.2	To the left of the "Game Trail" ski sign and a descending road is a rocky road, Kloser's Klimb. Climb up this briefly, then turn right and stay right as the flat and smooth Grand Traverse singletrack begins.
7.7	Cross a faint doubletrack.
8.8	Cross under the ski area boundary ropes, and start climbing.
9.1	Ride straight through an intersection. A sharp left leads to Wildwood.
9.3	Turn right on the unmarked Cougar Ridge Trail. There is a short climb near the beginning, then a long, fast downhill.
12.4	Stay right, passing a spur to an overlook.
12.6	American Flag overlook above Minturn. Descend steeply.
14.3	The Game Creek Trail merges in from the right.
14.8	End of the trail in a Minturn neighborhood. Descend to 4th Street.
15.0	Turn right on 4th Street.
15.3	(approx. mileage) Turn right on Minturn Road and follow this north. Cross a bridge over the Eagle River.
16.0	(approx. mileage) Turn right on Highway 24.
16.5	(approx mileage) Ride under I70 and turn right onto the bike path, crossing the Eagle River. Continue on the bike path along Gore Creek back to West Vail. At a park, begin riding on the South Frontage Road. Stay on the shoulder.
21.0	(approx. mileage) Back to the Lionshead parking. 🚲

VAIL MOUNTAIN DOWNHILL TRAILS
Ride Information

Vail Mountain offers a big variety of cross country and downhill trails. See Cougar Ridge, Grand Traverse to Mid-Vail Escape, Two Elk Creek, and The Game Trail, pages 142-148 for cross country rides. Lift tickets are available throughout the summer season for access to the top of Eagle's Nest if you prefer to skip the ride up the mountain. To ride Vail Mountain, park at the Lionshead parking structure. To get here drive west on the South Frontage Road 6/10th of a mile from Vail exit 176, and turn left just before the information center. Tickets and summer trail maps are available at the Lionshead ticket office. This office is located down the stairs from the parking structure and through the shopping area and right, near the base of the gondola.

Vail recommends downhill equipment on the black downhill trails due to the technical nature of these trails. No uphill traffic is permitted on these trails. They are quite rough from high speed and heavy use, not recommended for cross country riding.

Construction is happening near the base of Vail Mountain, so several trails may be closed, changed, or re-routed for a period of time.

Beginner and intermediate trails: (Good Cross Country Routes)

Upper Fireweed: Smooth connecter between Eagle's Nest and Mid-Vail. Great either direction. Easy singletrack.

Eagle's Loop: Right off the gondola, easy singletrack.

Gitalong Road: Gradual road up to Mid-Vail. Good beginner descent.

Vail Village Trail: Moderate road up to Eagle's Nest. Easy descent.

Upper Fred's Lunch: Mostly doubletrack, moderate descent from Mid-Vail.

Grand Traverse: Intermediate singletrack that traverses high above Vail's back bowls. An awesome trail!

South 6th Escape: Moderate old doubletrack.

Lion's Down: Moderate descent from right below the gondola, good as an uphill also. Mostly road, some singletrack at the bottom.

Mill Creek Road: A long, moderate climb to the Commando Run.

Advanced Trails:

Cougar Ridge: Descends from the Grand Traverse to Minturn. Mostly singletrack. Great ride.

The Game Trail: All singletrack, steep descent into Minturn. Great trail.

Commando Run: Short fun, singletrack connector to the Two Elk Trail.

High Noon Ridge: Mostly doubletrack descent to the Two Elk Trail.

Kloser's Klimb: A rocky and grueling old doubletrack climb to the top of Vail Mountain from Eagle's Nest.

Difficult Downhill only Trails: (Downhill Equipment Required)

Magic Forest: This trail starts just below the gondola terminal with a short hop over stair step rocks. It opens with big switchbacks that mirror the contour of the terrain. It dives into some trees in the middle section where there are some unique features to go over or around. The bottom opens up and then after a short stint on Cubs Way you can head over to Lower Fred's Lunch and reach the bottom.

Lower Fred's Lunch: A short singletrack connector between Magic Forest and Mane Lane.

Mane Lane: A short, challenging singletrack with some technical elements.

Old Nine Line: Form your impression of the Old 9 Line just by looking down it from the top. It's a steep, gnarly, technical ride for the most experienced riders. (Not for the faint of heart!) Old Nine Line falls on the steep, shady side on the mountain, which makes the dirt a bit more tacky. It provides varied terrain, it flows nicely, and there is a network of braided routes with a lot of possible transfers.

'94 Downhill: The 1994 World Cup Championship Downhill Race Course is a difficult combination of steep descents and technical singletrack that starts at Mid-Vail and descends to Golden Peak. ᘓᢛ

The Grand Traverse Trail, Vail Mountain

Commando Trail, Vail Mountain

Cougar Ridge Trail

COLORADO TRAIL: KOKOMO PASS

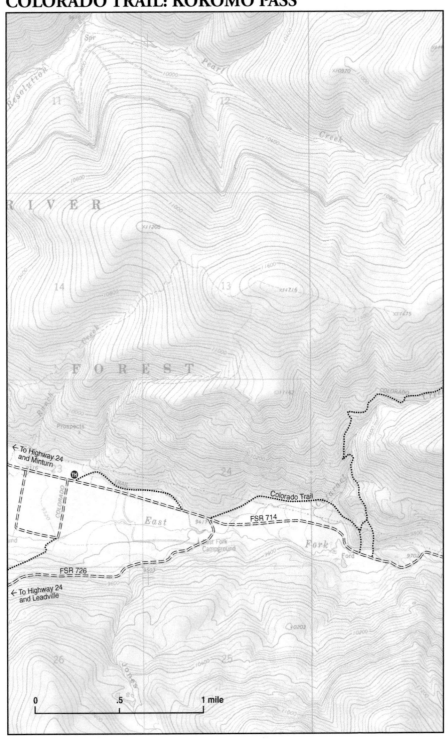

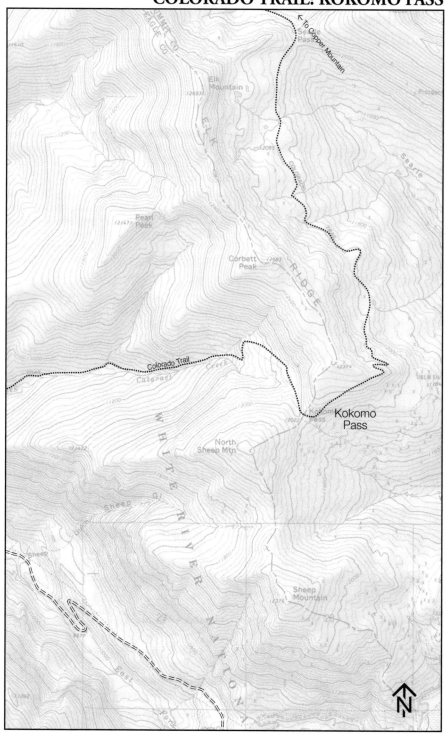

COLORADO TRAIL: KOKOMO PASS

← To Copper Mountain

Kokomo Pass

Colorado Trail

153

THE COLORADO TRAIL
Kokomo Pass
Ride Information

Description:

The Colorado Trail northeast from Camp Hale is a beautiful, all singletrack ride, with a remote wilderness feel to it. In the fall, listen for elk bugling, look for bear tracks, and enjoy the awesome fall colors of aspen groves and grassy meadows. There are great views of the Ten Mile Range from Kokomo Pass. As a climb, several sections are quite challenging and most riders can expect to walk some in the 1 ½ hours or so it will take to reach Kokomo Pass. The descent is fast and exciting. This ride can be combined with the Searle Pass section using a shuttle, see Colorado Trail, Searle Pass, page 100. Be sure to wear orange during the fall hunting seasons. From the Camp Hale Trailhead to Highway 24 is a fun addition of trail. It is located 1/10th of a mile down 714 and left ¼ mile toward the bunkers. Pickup the singletrack next to the bunkers.

Distance: 12 miles out and back, all singletrack except 1 mile old two track. 20 miles as a shuttle ride with the Searle Pass section, all singletrack except 1 mile of dirt road.

Time: 2-3 hours as an out and back, 4-5 ½ hours as a shuttle ride.

Overall Difficulty: Expert

Technical Skill: Expert

Aerobic Effort: High

Elevation: Top: 12,022' Gain: 2,522'

Season: July-early October

Usage: Light

Finding Route: Easy

Location: The Camp Hale Trailhead. To get here from Minturn (1.7 miles south of I70,) drive south about 15 miles on Highway 24 to Forest Service Road 702. Turn left and drive 1/10th of a mile. Turn right and parallel the highway for ½ mile, then turn left and drive 4/10ths of a mile to the junction of FS 702 and FS 714. Turn right and drive 2.2 miles on FS 714, passing several spurs, to the signed Colorado Trail and parking on the left. To get to the Camp Hale Trailhead from Tennessee Pass, drive north 2.9 miles on Hwy. 24 and turn right on the unsigned Forest Road 726. Follow FS 726 two miles to Forest Road 714, turn left and drive 7/10ths of a mile to the Colorado Trail trailhead on the right.

Maps: Latitude 40 Summit County Colorado Trails or Sky Terrain Summit, Vail, Holy Cross

Mileage Log:

0.0 Ride through the parking area onto the singletrack and turn immediately right. The trail rolls south up the valley, paralleling the road.

0.7 Roll back onto FS 714. Stay left, continuing up the valley.

0.9   Arrive at a road and trail intersection. Turn left onto the Colorado Trail singletrack and begin climbing. (FS 714 continues straight and FS 726 turns right to Hwy. 24.)

1.7   Cross Cataract Creek and descend to an intersection. Stay left on the Colorado Trail as a four-wheeler track and then a singletrack split off to the right. The trail climbs steeply on old doubletrack.

2.3   Ride straight ahead as a road merges in from the right.

2.4   Cross Cataract Creek again. If the creek is high, a log bridge is up the creek to the right. Climb steeply again.

2.5   Turn right onto the more used trail and traverse and climb more gradually. The trail has short steep sections that climb into the aspens and pines, then sustained steep climbing to reach the upper meadows.

5.0   Ride out into a beautiful high altitude meadow.

6.0   Summit Kokomo Pass! From here, turn around and zoom down to the valley, retracing your route back to your car. Or, continue three more miles and back on this rugged high altitude section to Searle Pass.

12.0   Back to the trailhead. ⚲

Summit of Kokomo Pass, Colorado Trail

BIKE SHOPS

Breckenridge

Great Adventure Sports 400 North Park, Breckenridge, next to City Market. 970-453-0333. greatadventuresports.com. Year round, quality full service shop. Sales, service, rentals. Right on the bike path!

A Racer's Edge 114 North Main St., Breckenridge. 970-453-0995 Full service and retail shop, rentals, trail information. Ellesworth & Rocky Mountain.

Mountain Outfitters, 112 S Ridge Street, Breckenridge. 970-453-2201. Sales, service and rentals. Outdoor gear, books and maps. Full retail shop.

Avalanche Sports 540 S. Main Street, Breckenridge. 970-453-1461. Rentals, repair, and demos. Santa Cruz, K2, Yeti.

Carvers 203 N Main Street, Breckenridge. 970-453-0132. Rentals.

Frisco

Wilderness Sports, 400 Main Street, Frisco. 970-668-8804. Sales, rentals, service. Voted best mechanic in Summit County. Outdoor supplies and climbing equipment.

High Trail Sports, 1121 N. Summit Blvd., Frisco. 970-668-3748. Sales, service, clothing, tours. Bianchi and LaMond.

Recycle Ski and Sport 842 North Summit Blvd. #34, Frisco. Between Safeway and Wal-Mart. 970-668-5150. New and used bikes and gear, repairs.

Pioneer Sports, Highway 9 next to Wal-Mart. 970-668-3668. Rentals.

Antlers, Highway 9, in front of Wal-Mart. 970-668-3152. Family bike rentals, clothing and accessories. Giant and K2.

Copper Mountain

Gravitee 0164 Copper Mountain, at the base area. 970-968-0171. gravitee.com. Sales, rentals, service; road and mountain bikes.

Vail

Vail Bike Tech, Lionshead Mall in Vail, in the Lifthouse Lodge. 970-476-5995. Sales, Service, rentals and tours.

Wheelbase 610 W. Lionshead Circle, Vail. 970-476-5799. Repairs and bike accessories. High end demos of Giant downhill, cross country and road bikes.

Minturn

Mountain Pedaler, 474 Main Street, Minturn, and 132 Broadway in Eagle. 970-827-5522. Sales, repairs, demos. Maverick, Litespeed, Intense, Kona and more! Open all year.

Edwards

Moontime Cyclery 0105 Edwards Village Blvd., #B105, Edwards. 970-926-4516. Full service bike shop, year round. Quality repairs, sales, parts, and clothing. Titus, Lenzsport, Scott USA, GT, Orbea.

The Kind Cyclist, 34323 Highway 6 in Edwards. 970-926-1260. Sales, service, custom frames and fitting. Road and mountain bikes.

Avon and Eagle-Vail

Avon Venture Sports, 51 Beaver Creek Place, Avon. 970-949-1318.
Sales, repairs, rentals, accessories. Friendly service! Vail pass tours.
Colorado Bike Service, 41149 Highway 6 and 24. Dowd Park Business
Park, Eagle-Vail. 970-949-4641. Sales, service, maps and rentals. Specialized,
Cannondale, Bianchi, Merlin, Giant.
Pedal Power 40784 Highway 6, Avon. 970-845-0931.
Sales and repairs. Moots, Trek, Fischer, Klein, Serotta, Look.

Frisco

Wilderness Sports, 400 Main Street, Frisco. 970-668-8804. Sales, rentals, service.
Voted best mechanic in Summit County. Outdoor supplies and climbing equipment.

Silverthorne and Keystone

Mountain Sports Outlet, 167 Meraly Way, Silverthorne. 970-262-2836. Large
selection of bike and gear. Santa Cruz, Klein, Intense, Trek, Specialized,
Gary Fisher.
Mountain View Sports, 22869 U.S. Highway 6 and Rasor Drive, Keystone.
970-468-0396. Rentals, service, Vail pass shuttle and coasting trips.

Eagle

Mountain Pedaler 132 Broadway in Eagle or 474 Main Street, Minturn.
970-827-5522. Sales, repairs, demos. Maverick, Litespeed, Intense, Kona and more!
Open all year.

Fairplay

High Alpine Sports Main Street and 9th, Fairplay. 719-836-0201. Repairs, bike and
outdoor gear and supplies.

Leadville and Buena Vista

Bill's Sport Shop, 225 Harrison Avenue, Leadville. 719-486-0739.
Bike supplies, gear, and maps. Small repairs.
The Trailhead 707 U.S. Highway 24 North, Buena Vista. 719395-8001. Sales,
repair, outdoor and bike gear, maps, books. Trek bicycles.

SHUTTLES AND BIKE TOURS

Vail Bike Tech Tours. Lionshead Mall, Vail. 970-476-5995. www.vailbiketech.com
Mountain View Sports. 22869 US Hwy. 6 & Rasor Dr., Keystone. 970-468-0396.
Vail Pass Tours
Colorado Bike Tours/ Wilderness Sports. 400 Main Street, Frisco. The only
liscensed guide service in the area! 970-668-8900. Coloradobikeandski.com.
Avon Venture Sports, 51 Beaver Creek Place, Avon. 970-949-1318.
Sales, repairs, rentals, accessories. Friendly service! Vail pass tours.
Mountain Wave 600 South Park Avenue, Breckenridge, 970-453-8305 and
220 Main Street, Frisco, 970-668-2759. Bike rentals, shuttle service. Will drop off or
pick up at any trailhead! Specialized FSR full suspension and specialized comforts.
High Trail Sports, 1121 N. Summit Blvd., Frisco. 970-668-3748. Sales, service,
clothing, tours. Bianchi and LaMond.

Buffeher Trail, Vail

The Colorado Trail, Horseshoe Gulch Section

About the Author

Holly Annala lives in Crested Butte Colorado with her husband, Rob Mahedy. She has spent all but two years of her life in Colorado. She grew up on a ranch in Durango, Colorado and has always loved the outdoors. Holly has been mountain biking for 18 years, has dabbled in racing, teaches mountain bike clinics for women in Crested Butte, and has written one previous mountain bike guide, Crested Butte Singletrack and Hartman's Rocks in Gunnison. She is happiest out on the trail and camping around the west. For questions or comments, please write her at hollyannala@yahoo.com. For information on her mountain bike clinics for women, visit Crested Butte Mountain Guides at crestedbutteguides.com.

Trail Notes

photo by Kurt Olesik

Vail Mountain